DISCARDED

THUNDER *on the* GULF

THUNDER on the GULF
OR
The Story of the Texas Navy

By
C. L. DOUGLAS

THE OLD ARMY PRESS

Copyright 1936
Turner Company

Old Army Press Edition 1973

The Cover Painting of Commodore Moore
and Officers of the Texas Navy
Painted by J. Hefter, c 1973 by Michael J. Koury

THE OLD ARMY PRESS

405 Link Lane
Fort Collins, Colorado 80521

INTRODUCTION

One year before Major General Jim Dan Hill wrote his excellent history of the Texas Republic's small navy, C. L. Douglas published *Thunder On the Gulf.* Both volumes today command premium prices in the first edition. Hill's work, *The Texas Navy*, was reprinted in 1962. In some ways, however, the book by Douglas is an even better one. Certainly the style in Douglas' *Thunder On the Gulf* is exciting. As the *first* book on the Texas Navy, it has long deserved reprinting. *Thunder On the Gulf* smells the acrid smell of black powder, and tastes the bitter taste of salt water. It is filled with adventures well told.

As an epilogue to this excellent seafaring tale, a rare article has been added. Better than any second-hand account, "The Dismasted Brig; or, Naval Life In Texas," allows the reader to almost experience the feeling of helplessness and destitution felt by the navy of Texas. Foresaken by its government, the navy was left to its own devices. How she fared is better understood in the words of one who lived through that low point of Texas' naval history.

Readers young and old alike will thoroughly enjoy C. L. Douglas' fine history of Texas' two navies. Percy St. John, through his article, "The Dismasted Brig," brings a personal, "first-hand" touch to the story. Indeed the Texas Navy's cannon made "Thunder On the Gulf."

Michael J. Koury
Editor - The Old Army Press

CONTENTS

Chapter I
   First Salvo 1

Chapter II
   Wasps of the Sea; The Privateers 11

Chapter III
   Gunpowder and Flour 18

Chapter IV
   The Capture of the Brig Pocket 24

Chapter V
   The Cruise of the Brutus 34

Chapter VI
   The Independence Strikes Her Colors 47

Chapter VII
   New Sail and New Hulls 53

Chapter VIII
   Off Yucatan 60

Chapter IX
   Under the Broad Pennant 69

Chapter X
   The Mutiny on the San Antonio 79

Chapter XI
   Pirates All 91

Chapter XII
   Death on the Fore-Yard 102

Chapter XIII
   Campeche 110

Chapter XIV
   Last Salvo 122

Epilogue 129

Chapter I

FIRST SALVO

The merchant schooner *San Felipe,* under full sail and with a fair wind behind, was beating in for Velasco, the Texas trading post at the mouth of the Brazos River.

She had wallowed up the Mexican Gulf from New Orleans; and although a vessel of commerce engaged in peaceful pursuits, she carried on this voyage two six-pound waist guns upon her deck, and her bulwarks were braced with bales of cotton.

Captain William A. Hurd, sailing as master under the registry of McKinney and Williams, merchants of Velasco and Quintana, was taking no chances—for he had aboard two passengers whom he did not care to have fall into Mexican hands during these critical days of 1835.

One was Stephen F. Austin. He was returning to his Texas colony after two years' imprisonment in Mexico, whither he had gone in a vain attempt to persuade that government to make an independent state of her Texas province.

The other was Don Lorenzo de Zavala, one-time private secretary to Santa Anna, the Mexican president, but now estranged from the imperious dictator because of a disagreement over policies. Either of these men, Austin or Zavala, would have been welcome prey for the Mexican gunboats then blockading the Texas seaports in an effort to force the rebellious colonists into paying excessive revenue levies.

Captain Hurd was worried, and before leaving New Orleans, where the two distinguished passengers had boarded the ship, he had made certain preparations. In addition to taking aboard the six-pounders and strengthening the bulwarks with cotton, he had obtained ample small arms for his crew, and he felt ready to meet eventualities.

The master did well to take such precautions, for as the *San Felipe* neared the home port that night—August 31, 1835—another boat lay at anchor off the harbor of Velasco. She was a trim-appearing craft . . . a rakish, low-lying sloop-of-war . . . with the words *Correo Mexicano* painted on her side. Even without the Mexican flag which fluttered from the mizzen, that was quite enough to identify her for what she was—the raider of the notorious Thomas M. "Mexico" Thompson, an English sea adventurer in the pay of Santa Anna's government.

Already "Mexico" Thompson had established for himself quite an unenviable reputation among the Anglo-Saxon colonists of Texas. Earlier in the year, after Colonel William B. Travis and a group of armed citizens had chased the customs officials out of Anahuac, Thompson had been sent with his sloop to put the fear of the Central Government into the hearts of the people in that town, but his methods of terrorism had been such that he had merely stirred to brighter flame the smouldering fires of rebellion.

And now, with the *Correo,* he lay off Velasco . . . waiting.

It was near four o'clock in the afternoon of September 1 that the watch of the Mexican raider sighted the approaching *San Felipe.* The merchantman was tacking in for the anchorage; and "Mexico" Thompson, seeing what she was about, called an order to Lieutenant Carlos O'Campo, his second in command.

"Get in to windward," he said, "and cut her out."

O'Campo hustled the crew and the sloop, almost immediately, got under way—slipping slowly out of her berth in an attempt to block the *Felipe* at the harbor mouth; the merchantman, meanwhile, clapping on all sail to make a run for it. The race started, while from the shore Thomas F. McKinney, one of the schooner's owners, anxiously watched the progress of the maneuvers.

Not many months before Messrs. McKinney and Williams had paid out nearly ten thousand hard-earned dollars for the vessel and, naturally enough, they had no desire to see her fall into the hands of the *Correo;* but, as the sloop began gaining to windward, McKinney knew that something had to be done, and that right speedily. Finally, in desperation, he turned to the crowd which had gathered on the wharf.

"We've got to go out and help her, boys," he shouted. "Who'll volunteer to go with me?"

"I'm your man!" said a bronzed hunter, just in from an expedition up the Brazos.

"Count on me," said another, a buck-skin shirted

gentleman who held a long squirrel rifle in the crook of his right elbow. "I'm fair spoilin' for a fight."

Other volunteers came forward—about fifty in all— and McKinney, without further formality, rushed them all aboard the *Laura,* a small steamer recently purchased by the firm.

Fortunately, the *Laura* already was under steam, and it required but a relatively short time for the vessel to warp alongside the hard-pressed *San Felipe.* The steamer hurriedly transferred the volunteers to the deck of the schooner and then, after making fast a tow-line, snaked the *San Felipe* into the anchorage, the reinforced crew standing ready at the rail with small arms.

The sail vessel was comparatively safe now, for it was unlikely that "Mexico" Thompson would dare follow through the harbor entrance, but McKinney had his blood up. As he watched the *Correo Mexicano,* still moving in to windward, he conferred briefly with Captain Hurd, Austin, and Zavala.

"If it's a fight they want," said the merchant, "they shall have it. But first, Mr. Austin, we're going to put you ashore . . . you've had enough of Mexican prisons for a while, I suspect. And you'd better go, too, Zavala. I imagine Santa Anna would like to have you with him again."

Stephen F. Austin protested, and so did Zavala, but at the insistence of McKinney they boarded the *Laura,* leaving the volunteers and the crew of the *San Felipe* to clear decks and organize for action. Another conference was held and it was decided that McKinney, by virtue of ownership, should take general command, with Hurd in charge of the sailors while Captain Hoskins and William Brown managed the waist guns.

Until 10 p. m. the *San Felipe* swung at anchor, the *Correo* moving slowly down to windward under a reefed mainsail, her tender leading the way. It became obvious now, from the movements of the enemy vessel, that a fight was coming, and the men of the *San Felipe* looked to their weapons and stood ready.

Apparently unaware that the schooner was armed, the tender for the Mexican sloop moved across the merchantman's stern, opening with a volley from small arms, but McKinney held his backwoods riflemen in check.

"Not yet! Not yet!" he shouted. "Wait for the sloop!"

The *Correo* was coming closer. There was a rattle of musketry from her deck by way of warning, and then Thompson spoke his opponent.

"Ahoy, the San Felipe!" came the cry from the Briton. "Stand by, and send your papers aboard!"

McKinney, cupping his hands to his mouth, shouted back his answer:

"You want our papers, eh . . . well, come and get 'em!"

Thompson didn't hesitate. He ordered O'Campo to give the Texans a warning shot with a six-pounder.

Boom! The ball screamed over the *San Felipe's* deck and spent itself in the sea.

"Mexico" Thompson waited. That warning shot. he was sure, would inform these merchant pirates that he meant business . . . but even as he waited Mr. Thompson received one of the major surprises of his maritime career.

"Give 'em two of the same!" shouted McKinney, and as the matches went to the vents of the waist guns two six-pound balls went thundering across toward the *Correo Mexicano,* one going high, the other striking the deck and scudding away into the water.

This was more than the Englishman had bargained for . . . having had no intimation that his opponent was armed . . . and, recovering from his surprise, he ordered another round from his own six-pounders. But too late —Captain Hurd had unsprung and cut his cable and the two ships were slowly drifting together.

Fifty yards . . . twenty-five . . . and then the *San Felipe's* crew let go with the small arms, raking the enemy's decks and silencing the waist guns. The *Correo* began to swing about, bearing away to leeward, and within a few minutes was out of range of the sharpshooters.

"We've got 'er on the run, boys," yelled McKinney. "Now let's give 'er a chase!"

Whereupon the *San Felipe* also swung about and headed for sea, but the *Correo,* being a fast sailor, was soon lost in the star-lit night . . . with "Mexico" Thompson standing on the after-deck, gently swearing good Mersey oaths.

Throughout the night the *San Felipe,* under full sail, followed on the course the enemy had taken. Dawn revealed the quarry far ahead, just a splotch of white sail on the horizon; and McKinney, helping keep the deck watch, saw little chance of overhauling her.

Then he sighted the *Laura,* coming up from astern. The little steamer, manned by every effective man in Velasco, was coming out to put a finger in the pie, and at the sight of her the merchant's heart leaped. There was still an opportunity to catch Thompson . . .

The *Laura,* her engine puffing and panting, came alongside.

"Throw us a line!" yelled McKinney. "We're going after 'em!"

"Over she comes!" came a voice from the steamer . . . and immediately a tow was made fast and the little steamer's paddle-wheels were turning away in the wake of the Mexican.

It was steam versus sail now, and within an hour the *Laura* had jockeyed the *San Felipe* within range of the *Correo Mexicano.*

"Clear for action!" ordered McKinney. "Man the guns, but give her a signal. Get your sharp-shooters ready, Hurd."

But the last command was unnecessary. With the signal gun, a high shot with one of the six-pounders, Thompson lost his nerve, though his guns were shotted and their vents primed. He didn't reply with so much as one answering salvo. Instead, he struck . . . and a wild cheer broke from the deck of the *San Felipe* as the Eagle and Snake of Mexico came fluttering down from the masthead.

Texas had won her first victory on the high seas . . . a merchantman against a man-o'-war . . . and a merchantman, at that, without a flag and without a government to back its actions . . .

McKinney now called for volunteers to board the prize, and although nearly every man on the *San Felipe* stepped forward, only three were chosen—Captain Hoskins, A. J. Harris and J. M. Shreve.

The longboat was lowered and the three went over with instructions to take charge of the *Correo* and send Captain Thompson aboard the victor with his papers.

"Damned if I do!" said Mexico Thompson, when the prize crew came on deck and explained McKinney's orders. "It's nothing short of piracy . . . that and nothing else . . . and every man on the schooner will have to answer, sooner or later, to the government. It's rebellion!"

Hoskins did the talking for the boarding party, while Shreve and Harris stood by with a pistol in each hand. Without ceremony, they ordered fifteen Mexican marines to get themselves below decks; then, after ordering Thompson and Lieutenant O'Campo into the longboat, they pulled off for the *San Felipe,* and Thompson took his papers with him.

Aboard the merchantman, Thompson stormed. He repeated to McKinney all that he had said to Hoskins. It was rank piracy, he said, and rebellion, and—since five of the *Correo's* crew had been killed—it was murder, too.

But that worried McKinney not at all. Rather, he congratulated himself that the *Felipe* had sustained only one casualty . . . one man slightly wounded.

There was one little difficulty, however. Now that the Texans had taken their first prize at sea they didn't know just what to do with it. Since, legally, Texas still was a province of Mexico, McKinney and all his men realized that they had committed an overt act of rebellion upon which, as Thompson forecast, they probably would be called to account.

Anyhow, the *Correo* was towed into the anchorage at Velasco, and there the matter was bridged over very nicely. That night the leading citizens of Velasco and Quintana held a mass meeting and decided that there was "some informality in the sailing papers of Thompson's ship," whereupon the Briton and all his crew were hastened off to New Orleans and turned over to United States authorities to face charges of "piracy on the high seas."

The captain and Lieutenant O'Campo actually were brought to trial before Judge Harper of the United States District Court, but the jury, after acquitting O'Campo, failed to agree in the case of Captain Thompson. Finally the court called a new trial for the skipper, whereupon the prosecution entered a motion for dismissal, apparently because the attorneys detected the weak spots in the charges brought by the Texans. Judge Harper, however, did send some of the lawyers to jail—for throwing ink wells during the progress of the argument.

Thus came to an end the first important sea engagement in the case of the Province of Texas versus the Republic of Mexico, forerunner of many a hard-fought battle yet to come.

Soon, those wasps of the sea, the privateers, would be hoisting sail and taking to the main under Letters of Marque and Reprisal granted by a provisional Texas government made up of Anglo-Saxon rebels—and those ships were to hold sea rovers as salty as any who ever staged a mutiny or hanged a man to a yard-arm.

History has dealt unfairly, and unjustly, with the Texan Navy; or, rather, the *two* navies of the Texas Republic—and as a result few people of this day are aware of the misery it caused Mexico, the prime purpose for which it was sent to sea.

Like the hornet, the Lone Star navy was ever small; but, again like the hornet, it had a stinger—and it placed that stinger in every port of the Mexican seacoast from Yucatan to Matamoras.

Chapter II

WASPS OF THE SEA; THE PRIVATEERS

Captain William Kidd, old Bluebeard, Blind Pew and similar "brethren of the coast" would have delighted in the situation which existed along the shores of the Mexican Gulf in 1835 and 1836.

Texas, not yet a Republic, but preparing to fire the opening gun in her struggle for independence from Mexico, was aware that since the seeds of rebellion had been planted the enemy might be expected not only by land, but by sea; and since it is through seaports that the lifeblood of any nation flows, the Provisional Government of Texas, during its formative period in 1835, gave early consideration to organization of a naval force to patrol the southern coastline.

No money being available to equip a land army, much less purchase ships, Provisional Governor Henry Smith and the General Council did the only thing that could be done under the circumstances. They recommended that certain gentlemen of the coastal region, principally men already in possession of sea-going craft, be issued Letters of Marque and Reprisal—papers which permitted the bearers to blockade any of the ports of Mexico and prey on the sea commerce of the enemy. It was, in a way, a system of legalized piracy—with the government stipulating that it should receive a share, usually twenty per cent, of all booty taken by these ocean rovers.

In this manner the ways were laid for the launching of the first Texas Navy.

One of the heroes of the fight with the *Correo Mexicano,* Captain William Hurd, was one of the first to clear port with a Letter of Marque among the papers in his cabin, but not on the *San Felipe.* That gallant little schooner, while chasing a Mexican sloop around Matagorda Bay, had gone aground near Paso Cavallo. The sloop, seeing the *Felipe's* difficulty, had returned to give her a broadside, but Hurd had put up such a stiff cannonading that the Mexican sloop stood off and finally abandoned the project. The *Felipe's* guns then were transferred to the schooner *William Robbins,* in which Master Hurd set out to harass the Mexicans.

As the *William Robbins* (the name was later changed) the new privateer distinguished herself but once. A group of Americans and Spanish-Americans, in preparation for the revolt that was about to break over Texas, had chartered the *Hannah Elizabeth* for gun running purposes.

The vessel loaded at New Orleans—with five hundred muskets, two cannon, and a supply of powder and ball—but while nearing the Texas coast, off the mouth of Matagorda Bay, she was overhauled by the Mexican gunboat *Bravo,* which forced a surrender without a fight.

The *Bravo* put a small prize crew aboard under command of Lieutenant Mateo, but these gentlemen were scarcely on the *Hannah Elizabeth's* deck before the gunboat was caught in the teeth of a norther and blown to sea. Fate then decreed that the *William Robbins* should appear on the scene—to recover the cargo of the *Hannah* and make prisoners of the *Bravo's* prize crew—an episode which virtually closed the career of the *Robbins,* under that name. Later, rechristened the *Liberty,* this same boat was to figure prominently in the first official Navy . . .

The lure of buccaneering has always held attraction for the venturesome, so in this Texas situation arrived many willing seamen, all anxious for Letters of Marque with which to seek a fortune under the new-made Texas flag. Various ships fitted out and put to sea, but this narrative will confine itself to a select few —merely to show how these ocean wasps, recruited to harass the mother nation, made their stingers felt from one end of the Mexican coast to the other.

A notable example was the *Thomas Toby,* named for the Texas agent at New Orleans. Skippered by Captain Hoyt, the ambitious *Toby* cruised up and down the Gulf, dropping anchor off Mexican ports and challenging the enemy to send out their best brigs for combat.

This privateer made one memorable journey down east coast in October of 1836, and although it didn't cause much damage, except to small enemy craft in the Gulf, its insulting challenges were left at most the principal Mexican ports—Matamoras, Tampico, Vera Cruz, Sisal, and as far south as Campeche, in Yucatan.

Shortly after the middle of the month the *Thomas Toby* ran in toward the Fort at Tampico and this, according to an account in a Texas newspaper of the day, is what occurred:

"She played her 'long tom' upon it for some time without, however, doing much damage, except frightening the good people of the town nearly out of their wits, who, supposing her to be the vanguard of the Texian navy, turned out en masse, repaired to the fort and along the river banks, determined to repel any hostile movement of the imaginary fleet. The commander of the privateer soon afterward trasmitted a challenge to the commandant of Tampico requesting a meeting with any armed Mexican vessel which might be in port; but receiving no answer within a reasonable time, she stood off and spoke the *Louisiana* (saying she was) determined to capture all Mexican property she fell in with."

And the *Toby* did take several prizes, like the one referred to in the *Telegraph and Register* published at Columbia, Texas.

"The *Thomas Toby*," said the *Register*, "has just sent into Galveston a very valuable prize, being a large fine brig, strongly built, and capable of being fitted out as a man-of-war, bearing guns heavier than any now in the Mexican Navy. She was captured off the coast of Campeachy and has on board 200 tons of salt. The *Tom Toby* when last seen was in hot pursuit of two Mexican schooners. This pursuit will undoubtedly prove successful as 'fortune ever favors the brave.' It is gratifying to reflect that our flag flaunts over one brave band whose dauntless spirits delight to career with the 'stormy petrel' over the tossing billows where danger lights the path to glory and to fame."

Sometimes, however, these bold fellows on 'the tossing billows' did not get their just share of the loot taken. Being anxious to attend to as much business as possible on a single cruise, the privateer would send a prize into Galveston in escort of another vessel while it remained in the hunting waters to snare another victim.

Something of this is brought out in an item published by the Houston *Star* under the caption "Cheap." It follows:

"A portion of the flour captured on the prize schooner *Progresso* was put up at auction and sold for $1 a sack of 220 pounds! The committee appointed to procure supplies for our volunteers were the purchasers, and no one bid against them. The *Civilian* says, "We can well afford to carry on war while the enemy furnishes us with supplies at such liberal terms." Now, we fear, the brave fellows who captured the *Progresso* are the sufferers in this instance, and if this cargo has sold at one-tenth of its value, it is their loss and not that of the enemy, since they are entitled to the prize money."

The *Toby* did a signal service in the cause of Texas against Mexico, but since the vessel was a privateer, and continued operations as such even after organization of the first official Texas Navy, Captain Hoyt apparently did not see fit to make any official reports to the Secretary of Navy. Thus first-hand accounts of the thunder her "Long Toms" raised on the Gulf are sadly lacking, except for the few brief accounts in the journals of the day. Most of the privateers neglected to make reports and perhaps that is one reason why the provisional government finally decided to call in the Letters of Marque, or as many of them as possible. It may be that the government suspected that it was losing a part of that twenty per cent "cut."

The *Toby* did make one trip by official order—sailing for Havana to pick up a couple of brass cannon which the ladies of that city had purchased as a gift for the Texas Republic, but it appears that delivery in Texas was delayed for some reason. The guns were still aboard the privateer when she went to Davy Jones' locker off Galveston during a storm in October of 1837.

The *Terrible,* Captain John M. Allen, was another of the Texas privateers that baited the Mexicans up and down the coast. As in the case of the *Toby,* little remains of her record, but that little indicates that she tried to live up to her name. Contemporary newspaper accounts disclose that Allen made several captures off Campeche banks, the most notable prize being the Mexican sloop *Matilda,* which furnished a cargo of provisions to the Texas revolutionists.

But even while the sea wasps were sailing the Mexican Gulf in quest of gold and glory, the first Texas Navy was born.

During the first two months of 1836 . . . even before the signing of the Declaration of Independence . . . the Provisional Government, through its naval secretary, Robert Potter, began drafting plans for the official fleet. The privateers, worrying the Mexicans through calls at first one port and then another, doubtless prevented many Mexican troop movements by sea, but the Provisional Government was looking ahead to the day when stronger protectionary measures would be needed to bolster the new government then in formation.

And so, with money raised from private sources, four vessels were purchased and put into commission—first the *Liberty* (once the *William Robbins*); then the *Independence,* the *Invincible,* and the *Brutus*.

The first commands of these vessels, in the order named, were given to Jeremiah Brown, William Brown, Charles E. Hawkins and William Hurd. A fifth boat, the *Flash,* still operating under Letter of Marque, was captained by Luke A. Falvel.

The *Invincible,* built in Baltimore for the African slave trade, was the fastest and strongest of the lot. She carried eight guns, two of which were eight-pounders. The *Independence* and the *Brutus* each mounted eight smaller pieces, and the *Liberty* four.

With this strength—twenty-eight guns against the combined sea power of Mexico—the first official Texas Navy set out to raise its own particular peal of thunder on the Gulf.

And just in time—the Alamo was about to fall, independence was in the making, and soon San Jacinto would be fought and won. At this critical moment General Sam Houston's army could ill afford to be worried by threats of invasion by sea. It devolved upon the Navy, though pitifully small, to keep the south coast clear and prevent Santa Anna, the Mexican president, from landing reinforcements.

How well that small navy succeeded, and with what spirit, is best explained in the stories which have to do with some of its encounters.

Chapter III

GUNPOWDER AND FLOUR

Off the port of Sisal, far down the east coast of Mexico, lay a four-gun schooner-of-war.

Slowly she cruised up within range of the shore fortifications, her single-star flag fluttering from the peak as if in defiance of the gunners behind the walls, but not a match touched fuse.

"The Texians again!" muttered the *coronel* in command of the shore batteries. He shrugged his shoulders and let the challenge pass.

"It's no use . . . they won't fight," said Captain William S. Brown. He barked an order, and the Texas schooner-of-war *Liberty* swung about and stood off a few points to sea.

The game, apparently, was over for the day, but at that moment—

"Sail ho!" sang the lookout. "Schooner on the weather quarter!"

The captain gave the lookout ample time to use his glass and then: "What do you make her?" he asked.

"Flies the Mexican flag, sir—an' I'd say, by her looks, she's the *Pelicano*."

Captain Brown lost no time.

"Man the guns . . . stand by for action!"

The *Pelicano* she was. Captain Perez had cleared her from New Orleans on February 25, 1836, and she carried a cargo of flour consigned by Zachari and Company to the Mexican government. With favorable winds the *Pelicano* had made a fair run down the coast to lift Sisal on March 3, the day after Texas independence had been declared . . . though, of course, it would be a fortnight before news of that momentous event would reach this corner of the world.

The Mexican tacked in for the anchorage, but whether because he failed to realize *Liberty's* identity, or because of sheer bravado—for the *Pelicano* was carrying three brass cannon and a well-armed crew—Captain Perez headed straight for the Texan.

Brown, his men at battle stations, let him come; and then, when the range had narrowed, he put a volley of grape across the *Pelicano's* deck. The Mexican, seeing she was in for a fight, even if the action was taking place under the shadow of Sisal's fort, replied in kind, but the shot flew wild and went high of the *Liberty's* deck.

Captain Perez evidently had been expecting assistance from the shore guns, with the help of which Captain Brown might have been forced to put to sea, but for some unexplained reason the batteries of the fortifications failed to repsond.

Perez, at last realizing that he hoped in vain, tried to put about and stand off after another ineffectual volley, but Brown—who had got in another telling shot, had him, . . . and Perez knew it.

The *Pelicano* hove to and struck her colors.

Thus far there had been no casualties on either side, and in this both skippers found cause for self-congratulation—Perez because he had escaped so easily, and Captain Brown because he considered the schooner a prize easily taken.

Seizing the trumpet, the Texan spoke the enemy and advised that he was sending a prize crew aboard and, after receiving an acknowledgment from the *Pelicano,* Brown tolled off three men to board her.

Seaman James O'Connor was delegated to lead the party, which took off in the longboat and headed for the Mexican while the *Liberty's* crew, equipped with small arms, stood at the rail to cover the boarders. O'Connor and his men pulled alongside and went up the ladder. Then the fun started.

The *Pelicano,* as a precautionary measure, was carrying on this voyage a company of twenty Mexican marines, all double armed with muskets, and as the *Liberty's* party came over the side, one of these gentlemen concluded that perhaps, after all, the day was not entirely lost.

He raised a musket to fire, but before he could pull the trigger Seaman O'Connor, who had come aboard with a pistol in his hand, knocked him over with a well-aimed shot.

Pandemonium broke loose on the *Pelicano's* deck. Some of the other marines ran for cover, others raised their muskets prepared to participate in what they believed a promising fight, and although some let go random shots as nervous fingers slipped from the trigger guards, the boarding party escaped unscathed.

The Texans could have clambored over the rail and into the longboat lying alongside, but instead they preferred to stand their ground, each of the three with a pistol in either hand—and when the melee was over and order had been brought out of chaos, seven dead Mexican marines lay stretched on the *Pelicano's* deck.

Naturally, the firing had occasioned alarm on the *Liberty,* but before Brown could so much as launch a boat to go to the aid of the prize crew, the crisis had passed and O'Connor had the situation well in hand.

The *Pelicano,* an inventory disclosed, was carrying five hundred and fifty barrels of flour, and a quantity of potatoes and apples—provisions enough to allow Santa Anna's troops to march many a mile on their bellies—but now all this foodstuff would go down Texan instead of Mexican throats.

After taking prisoner the officers and the crew of the enemy, and setting them ashore, Captain Brown of the *Liberty* appointed a select group of seamen to take the *Pelicano* in charge and sail her to Texas with her cargo. The vessel stood off from Sisal that night and took a course northward with the flour which Mr. James Zachari of New Orleans had sold to the Mexican army.

But it was not until the prize reached Matagorda Bay that the full extent of her cargo was known.

In attempting to cross the bar at the entrance of the Bay the *Pelicano,* obviously under-manned, ran on a reef and was wrecked. Neither the members of the prize crew nor the citizens living along the shore gave a tinker's damn about saving the enemy schooner—though it might have been used later as an arm of reprisal—but they did want the flour that she carried.

While the schooner was pounding out her ribs on the reef, one longboat after another visited her to take off the cargo—the five hundred and fifty barrels containing the "staff of life" in powdered form.

Then one of the landing crews dropped a barrel, and as the staves fell apart something else rolled out—a smaller keg which had been hidden in the flour.

It didn't take the Texans long to determine what that keg contained, and they rejoiced as they examined one barrel after another and found that each contained a similar keg . . . at least nearly all.

Besides a goodly supply of flour, which would make many a loaf for the Texan army, the Mexican government, in losing the cargo of the *Pelicano,* had provided that same army with enough gunpowder to fill many a cannon and musket.

Even General Sam Houston was elated when the news became general, and he issued a proclamation to inform the people of the good fortune that had been visited upon them through the enterprise of Captain Brown and the men of the *Liberty.*

Of course, James Zachari, the New Orleans consignee, was desperate. The company could ill afford to lose that much flour, even if it did go to a cause popular in Louisiana. He was in business for himself, and not in the interest of Texan liberty, and when he heard of the sad fate which had overtaken the Mexican sloop he issued a statement denying that any gunpowder had been mixed in with the flour.

This statement came at last to the ears of the *Liberty's* commander, and when he reached Galveston in the early part of May he issued the following reply:

"I am informed that J. W. Zachari denied that there was any powder on board schooner *Pelicano*. I do assure you that there was 280 kegs; whether he knew it or not, I am unable to say. In addition to the above quantity, there were a number stowed in barrels of apples, potatoes, etc. I have found a number of letters on the prize which proved the above fact. I feel it to be my duty to state these facts in regard to the powder. There was no mention of it on the manifesto. My situation requires that I should keep a constant lookout and when I see the Mexican flag flying, I shall either take it or be taken. I can not fly from a Mexican, and will not."

And that is the story of the Texan Schooner-of-War *Liberty*, a tale of flour and gunpowder, for she went no more to the Mexican Main. A short time later, under command of Captain George Wheelwright, whom Commodore Charles Hawkins had appointed to succeed Brown, she sailed to New Orleans for repairs. When the work was done the poverty-stricken Texas government couldn't pay—and one of her "ships of the line" went on the auction block.

Captain Brown, who had been relieved from command because of some difference with Commodore Hawkins, later was issued another commission, but he never used it. He died in New Orleans before he could get another boat.

But even during the time when William Brown was looking after the sea commerce off Sisal his elder brother, Jeremiah, was attending to similar business further north. Jeremiah Brown commanded the *Invincible*, best ship on the list of the first Texan Navy.

Chapter IV

THE CAPTURE OF THE BRIG POCKET

The Mexican brig *Bravo,* lately called the *Montezuma,* swung idly at her chains a few miles off the port port of Matamoras.

The captain, nervously pacing his quarter-deck, swore eloquent Spanish oaths as he awaited the return of his tender—long overdue from the mouth of the Rio Grande.

A hell of a time to lose a rudder—just when engaged in the business of holding all shipping in the Matamoras anchorage, a move intended to prevent the rebellious Texans from learning that the Mexican army had plans for landing a division of two thousand men at Copano Bay, on the south Texas coast!

The captain could think of more pleasant things, but even as he fretted a strange sail appeared on the horizon. He squinted through the glass, then handed it to the second officer, asking him what he made of the stranger.

"Quien sabe," said that worthy, but nevertheless he kept an anxious eye on the approaching sail, for those were perilous times on the Gulf of Mexico. On this day, the tenth of April, 1836, anything might come to pass—for the rebel Texians, incensed over the slaughter at the Alamo and the massacre of Col. J. W. Fannin's men at La Bahia, were preparing for that one great thrust which, when it came at San Jacinto on the twenty-first of the same month, would assure Texas liberty from the rule of Santa Anna.

The Dictator would be in need of those troops which were to be landed at Copano. The coast must be blockaded—and now the *Bravo* had lost her rudder! Small wonder that the captain fumed.

The strange sail came nearer, and the Mexican officers wondered when they saw that she carried no colors. They continued to wonder when they saw through their glasses that the stranger had dropped a longboat, which was taking off in the direction of the crippled *Bravo*.

In the stern of the longboat sat a young officer, Lieutenant William H. Leving. He had orders to check the brig and see what she was up to, and those orders had come from Captain Jeremiah Brown, commander of the strange sail—the Texan Schooner-of-War *Invincible*.

The captain of the *Bravo* received his visitor with all the politeness usually accorded a guest, but at the same time he was suspicious. Why hadn't the stranger broke her colors? He wondered about that—and secretly gave orders to slip the *Bravo's* cable, which allowed the ruderless brig to drift slowly toward the mouth of the Rio Grande and Matamoras.

Meanwhile, on the *Invincible*, Captain Jere Brown had been watching through his glasses, and when he saw what the Mexican was about, he gave orders to close in. With Lieutenant Leving aboard the enemy, Brown didn't like the situation, and he said as much to the first officer.

The *Bravo,* incapable of being steered, ran in across the bar—then went aground. It was at this moment that Jeremiah Brown went into action. Tacking the *Invincible* in, he hove to within easy range and let go two broadsides into the hull of the Mexican. He ordered the gunners to reload, then gave the helpless craft two more of the same; in a few minutes, reducing the *Bravo* to little more than wreckage.

Meanwhile the crew had gone overboard, taking Lieutenant Leving with them. He was never to return to his ship . . . because, at a later date, he was to be adjudged a pirate and shot at the orders of Santa Anna.

The *Invincible,* her job well done, now stood off and filled away, for the lookout had just discerned another sail approaching.

Captain Brown, the flush of battle upon him, saw in the newcomer an easy prey and so, breaking out the "single star of the West," he ordered chase. The stranger, taking the hint and knowing herself to be in waters where many skippers carried Letters of Marque, ran a bit before the wind, then hove to and unfurled the Stars and Stripes from her main peak.

Brown tacked his ship, ran close to the windward, and spoke the vessel, which proved to be the brig *Pocket* of Boston, Captain Elijah Howes commanding. She was, Howes explained, 13 days out of New Orleans with an assorted cargo consigned by M. de Lizardi and Company for the port of Matamoras.

The fact that the *Pocket* admitted her destination as an enemy port was quite enough for the skipper of the *Invincible*. He sent off a prize crew in the longboat, to hoist the Texas flag on the *Pocket's* mast and to order the captain aboard the *Invincible* with his papers.

"This is an outrage, sir," protested Howes, as he came up the ladder, "and I warn you that proper complaint shall be made to the United States government."

"That," replied Captain Brown, "will be quite all right . . . in due time, but I must remind you that Texas is at war with the central government of Mexico and that I find you about to enter an enemy port with a cargo of goods for the enemy. We'll check you over."

And check he did—finding, among other things, dispatches to Santa Anna, and a manifest that did not jibe with the cargo, which was made up of powder, ammunition and provisions for the Mexican army.

The Texans also were delighted to find two old friends among the passengers of the brig—none other than Captain Thomas M. Thompson and Lieutenant Carlos O'Campo, who had commanded the *Correo Mexicano* when that vessel was taken by the merchantman *San Felipe* off Velasco anchorage the previous August. These gentlemen had recently been in jail at New Orleans on a charge of piracy, and were now returning to Mexico preparatory to going to sea once more against the Texas Republic. Now they had fallen, so to speak, from the frying pan into the fire.

Jeremiah Brown smiled to himself over this piece of news, for he reasoned that Captain William A. Hurd would be mighty glad to see this pair. Captain Hurd, commanding the Texan schooner-of-war *Brutus,* lying at the moment off Galveston, had skippered the *San Felipe's* crew on the day that "Mexico" Thompson and O'Campo had struck the *Correo Mexicano's* flag in answer to a couple of six-pound shot.

In the eyes of Captain Brown many things were wrong with the brig *Pocket*. Second Mate Sommers held a commission in the Mexican Navy and was carrying papers from the Mexican consulate at New Orleans; two other passengers, named Hogan and Taylor, likewise were holders of Mexican Navy commissions; and then—to cap the climax—a descriptive map of the Texas coast was found among the ship's papers!

With all that, Captain Brown hardly needed the information offered by a passenger that the *Pocket*, on her return trip, was supposed to transport Mexican troops to the Texas coast. So he took charge of the brig as a legal prize, and two days later set sail with her for Galveston.

Captain Hurd of the *Brutus* apparently *was* glad to contact once more his old enemies of the *Correo Mexicano*. According to the report which the U. S. charge d'affaires at Galveston made the following year to the Texas government, some of the more "distinguished" visitors were turned over to Hurd and Lieutenant Damon of the *Brutus* immediately after arrival of the prize in port.

The charge alleged that Lieutenant Damon stripped O'Campo and Hogan, streched them over an eighteen-pound cannon, and had a member of the *Brutus* crew give them a couple of dozen with the cat-o'-nine-tails.

Then, just to carry the fun a little further, he had the yardarm braced and the order given to:

"Call all hands . . . we're going to hang some pirates."

According to the report, Damon actually had ropes placed about the necks of some of the prisoners, but in the end he contended himself with clapping the lot—Hogan, Taylor, Sommers, Murje, and O'Campo—in double irons for a period of three weeks.

Meantime, the crews of the *Invincible* and the *Brutus* busied themselves with the work of unloading the large stock of provisions carried by the *Pocket*. In a few days those eatables would come in handy, for the Texas army worked up a sizeable appetite during the process of whipping Santa Anna's forces at the battle of San Jacinto on the 21st of April . . . after which they fed heartily on the *Pocket's* stores.

On April 24, twenty-one days after the capture, Captain Howes and his men were allowed to proceed to New Orleans in another boat. The captain, angry over the loss of his ship and cargo, departed making threats that immediately he reached New Orleans he intended denouncing the *Invincible's* crew as pirates—and he did.

When the news of the capture became general there was great excitement in New Orleans, a town always friendly to the Texas cause, and flurries of this same excitement later swept through other seaports of the United States.

Had the *Invincible* been guilty of piracy, or had the *Pocket* violated the neutrality laws by running contraband? That was a question which brought out much discussion.

Meanwhile, the *Invincible* had lifted anchor at Galveston and had rolled down to New Orleans. She came up the river to find the attention of most of the town centered on her. Both Captain Howes and the Louisiana State Marine and Fire Insurance Company, insurers of the *Pocket's* cargo, had asked Commodore A. J. Dallas, commander of the U. S. Gulf Squadron, to arrest the Texas schooner as a pirate.

William Bryan, Texas agent in the Crescent City, had heard talk of this, and he went post-haste to the *Invincible* with orders for her to up-anchor and put to sea. Captain Brown had gone ashore the previous night and was out of the city at the time but the second in command, heeding the agent's warning, got under way immediately.

Bryan then returned to his office and wrote a letter to David G. Burnet, president of the Texas Republic, explaining that plans were afoot for seizure of the vessel by the United States marshal, and that he had acted to prevent a loss which would have served as a severe blow to Texas.

The *Invincible* sailed down the Mississippi—but too late.

She had scarce passed to sea before she was overtaken by the U. S. Sloop-of-War *Warren* and forced to return. The crew was landed under arrest and, with the cheers of the populace ringing in their ears, marched down Canal Street to the jail. The captain, hearing of the difficulty, hurried back to New Orleans and surrendered. Thomas Toby and Bros., a merchant marine firm always friendly to Texas put up his bail.

About a week later the trial was held, and it was brought out in testimony that a part of the *Pocket's* cargo was, indeed, contraband; therefore the Texan crew could not be guilty of piracy.

Released from custody, they made the welkin ring that night in the Vieux Carre, and somebody donated free tickets for a theater.

Then more difficulty. Captain Howes again attempted to have the crew arrested and brought to trial, but again Thomas Toby came to the rescue. The firm, for which a famous Texas privateer once had been named, bought the *Pocket* for $35,000, and then spent an additional $8,000 paying off damage claims filed by the officers and the crew.

But even that wasn't an end of the matter. The insurance company sued Captain Brown, asking $8,000 for the cargo that the heroes of San Jacinto had eaten —but there is no record to show that the company received settlement.

Then the United States government, whose flag had been violated, presented more than $12,000 worth of damage claims filed by passengers and members of the *Pocket's* crew, a business finally settled by treaty, at a cost of $11,750 to the Texas government.

But to return to the sea—

After her release at New Orleans the *Invincible* went on coast patrol duty, though she didn't have a great deal to do owing to the fact that the poverty-stricken Mexican navy was laid up temporarily.

In June of 1836 she was ordered to Velasco to take aboard General Antonio Lopez de Santa Anna, whom the Texan government had decided to release. The Mexican president, captured at San Jacinto, was to be taken to Vera Cruz on the Texas schooner, but after he came aboard plans had been changed, and Santa Anna was forced to remain awhile in Texas.

So the *Invincible,* taking advantage of the inaction on the part of the Mexican Navy, dropped anchor off Velasco bar, to laze in the sun.

Meanwhile, down in New Orleans, the friends of Texas still were making much of the *Pocket* incident, chiefly through publication of public broadsides in which they criticized the insurance company, M.de Lizardi and Company, and everybody connected with the operation of the brig.

One of these, published over the signature of Samuel Ellis, accused the insurance firm of being a tool for Santa Anna's agents. It was addressed to the president of the company, and it ended on this note:

"Your publication of the Protest was unnecessary and oppressive. It bears upon the face of it its own refutation, and that it was obtained for special purposes. The enthusiastic devotion of thirteen millions of freemen, gazing with admiration at the desperate valor of a handful of men devoting themselves to 'Liberty or Death', and disputing inch by inch the possession of their soil against a population of eight millions, is an argument that will answer a thousand protests obtained by Mexican influence.

"I will now leave you to your own reflections, with

this advice, that you act up to the honorable character you have thus far sustained. Shake off the shackles that your official station has imposed upon you, and shew to your fellow-citizens, that no pecuniary emolument can induce you to aid directly or indirectly, a cause predicated upon the indiscriminate slaughter of those who are endeared to us by every tie that can bind man to man—who are 'flesh of our flesh, and bone of our bone."

Chapter V

THE CRUISE OF THE BRUTUS

The Texas Schooner-o'-War *Brutus,* tugging at her chains in the mouth of the Rio Grande, was in trouble.

Outside the anchorage, maintaining vigilant blockade, lay the Mexican Brig-of-War *Vencedor del Alamo,* a ship of superior armament.

Captain William A. Hurd, who had sailed down from Texas on a scouting voyage only to find himself bottled in the Rio Grande, might have risked a run and a fight, if he had followed his own inclinations, but he felt that the effort might not be worth the risk, for the Texas Republic had no ships to lose at this critical stage in her efforts to preserve the independence so lately won on the field at San Jacinto.

It was well, perhaps, that the impatient *Brutus* remained in her cove—for the *Vencedor del Alamo,* having an important mission to perform, was prepared to show more fight than usually displayed by a Mexican vessel. Her job was to cover the operations of three Mexican schooners—the *Watchman,* the *Comanche,* and the *Fanny Butler*—while they landed on the Texas coast provisions for that portion of the Mexican army which had escaped the slaughter at San Jacinto.

If *Vencedor* could keep *Brutus* bottled in the bay all might go well and the stores be put ashore—but as events turned out, the Mexican, as she swung at anchor that hot day in July, 1836, was playing in vain the role of watchdog.

The *Vencedor* didn't know it yet, but her three schooners already were in Texas hands, and had been since the middle of June.

The *Watchman* had been the first captured. While lying in Copano Bay on June 2, waiting for a signal before landing her supplies, she had been sighted by a scouting party of twenty Texas Mounted Riflemen under command of Major Isaac Burton, then employed in scouting the coast in hope of contacting strays from the routed Mexican army.

The Major, who had a sense of humor, decided upon trickery. Leaving the horses with a detail, he signaled the *Watchman* to send in a boat, which she did. Burton then took into custody the landing party of five, manned the longboat with sixteen of his own men, and rowed back to the *Watchman,* whose surprised skipper surrendered without a show of fight.

Burton now gave orders for the captain to sail around to Velasco, but the vessel became becalmed and had to remain in Copano until the 17th of the month, during which time the *Comanche* and the *Fanny Butler* put in an appearance. Burton then resorted to a little pistol persuasion, forced the *Watchman's* captain to lure the skippers of the other craft aboard, and demanded a complete surrender. Thus, a company of twenty Mounted Riflemen won a victory at sea and found themselves in possession of three enemy vessels, which they took around to Velasco in high glee.

The little port celebrated in appropriate style, and

thereafter Major Burton and his twenty Rangers were known as the Texas Horse Marines.

But to return to the *Vencedor del Alamo* ("Conqueror of the Alamo") and the *Brutus*—

Captain Hurd had sent word of his plight to Captain Jeremiah Brown, still lazing off Velasco with the *Invincible,* but it was not until July 4 that the expected relief came. The *Invincible* then arrived in tow of the armed steamer *Ocean,* whereupon the *Vencedor del Alamo* rapidly filled away and set a course for Vera Cruz.

Jere Brown gave chase, following all the way to Vera Cruz, where he sent in a challenge to the *Vencedor* to come out and fight, but the commander of the Mexican declined the invitation, saying that he didn't have a proper crew, and besides, they hadn't been paid. Some other time, perhaps.

The *Invincible* swung about and returned to Texas, and later in the month sailed to New York for repairs.

There, she barely escaped being sold for debt, but after receiving the needed renovations managed to get away. She made Galveston, March 14, 1837, to be joined shortly by the *Brutus* which, absent without leave, also had been to New York and also had barely managed to clear port without being sold for debt.

Captains Brown and Hurd found the naval station and the officers of the fleet in mourning. The senior officer, Commodore Charles E. Hawkins, was dead, and the following announcement and General Orders had appeared in the February 28th issue of the Columbia Telegraph:

"It is with the most sincere sorrow that we are called upon to notice the decease of our gallant Commodore Charles E. Hawkins, who departed this life in New Orleans, on the 12th instant. At the most gloomy and discouraging period of our eventful struggle for national existence, he offered his service to our infant country, and continued to serve her, through good and evil report, up to his decease, with the same disinterested and undeviating fidelity. A more gentlemanly or chivalrous spirit never graced a quarter deck—and his loss will be deplored, and his memory respected by his gallant comrades of the navy, so long as merit in the naval profession claims esteem.

General Orders
Navy Department,
Columbia, February 26, 1837.

"That all due honor may be paid to the memory of the gallant and chivalric subject of the foregoing notice, it is hereby required that every commander of a squadron, single vessel, station, or naval depot shall, upon receipt of this order cause the colors to be lowered to half mast until sunset, and fire at noon a salute of thirteen guns. And all officers are required to wear crepe on the left arm for the space of thirty days, as a further testimony of their respect for their deceased brother in arms. By order of the President, S. Rhoads Fisher, secretary of the Navy."

In April the Department, displeased with certain actions on the part of the commanders—to wit: the capture of the Brig *Pocket* by Brown, and Hurd's unauthorized voyage to New York, made a few changes in the navy. Captain Henry L. Thompson supplanted Brown as commander of the *Invincible,* and James D. Boylan was instructed to take the quarter deck of the *Brutus.*

About the same time Secretary Fisher, feeling that his health was not all that it should be, decided that a sea voyage would be of great benefit. Accordingly, he ordered the two schooners to prepare for a cruise, and when they filled out from Galveston on June 10, 1837 the sea gear of the secretary was aboard the *Invincible.* The fleet, two vessels strong, was off for the Mexican main.

The ships sailed first to the mouth of the Mississippi River, but not finding any stray Mexican boats about, decided to part company temporarily and make a rendezvous at the Isle of Mugeres, on the tip of Yucatan.

Arriving there to find the inlets swarming with pirogues (small schooner canoes) they stripped all these craft of their sails and provisions, then wrecked or burned them. A few days later, overhauling a larger boat loaded with logwood, the *Invincible* took her in charge.

Captain Thompson, obviously, couldn't use the logs, but since they were being carried on a Mexican vessel—and since his chief mission was to worry Mexicans—he promised to let the Mexican off upon payment of a $600 ransom. The log hauler paid and Thompson split the proceeds among the crew of his own boat.

The two rovers then dropped down to Sisal, cannonading the place for three hours just as a reminder that they were on the job—and then, owing to the destitute condition of the vessels, in the way of rigging, the commanders thought it prudent to haul off.

"Had we had spare rigging, with which we could have repaired in case of sustaining damage, we could have easily taken the town," Captain Thompson reported later to the department.

Pirate-like, the two schooners-of-war, then went rolling up and down the coast.

The men made repeated landings, burning to the ground eight or nine villages, some of them of considerable size; and on one of these occasions Secretary Fisher—now reported in fine health and spirits—had a rather narrow escape.

He and Captain Boylan of the *Brutus* had landed at one of the towns, with a boat's crew of six, to obtain a supply of fresh water.

They hauled the boat up on the beach and, not expecting trouble, moved in a body toward the town, leaving their muskets in the boat. A troop of Mexican cavalry chanced to be in the village at the time and, seeing the strangers approach, the cavalrymen mounted their horses and charged.

As luck would have it the Texans had not progressed more than 200 yards from the boat, and as the twenty troopers charged out of the village, they turned and ran toward the beach. They reached the boat in safety, but even then they might have been sabered before they could pick up their muskets had not Secretary Fisher happened to have a pistol by him. While the sailors were securing their arms, Fisher turned and fired at the horsemen, dropping one from his sadle. The rest of the troop scattered and retreated.

At another time the boatswain of the *Brutus* and several men were out in the longboat pursuing a piroque when night overtook them. Landing at a small village, and the crew being dry, the boatswain roused the Alcalde from his sleep and laid the town under contribution with threats to burn the place to the ground. Fifty dollars being raised, the Texans spared the village and took their departure early in the morning.

The roistering navy, finding no more worthy prey along shore—the Mexican fleet lying for the moment unmanned at Vera Cruz—then set a course for Alacran Island; and there Thompson, new to full command and growing more arrogant with his men every day, involved himself in a situation which, eventually, was to result in his dismissal from the fleet.

First, the *Invincible* and the *Brutus,* beating up from Campeche, overhauled and took two prizes, both by the simple method of firing signal guns and sending aboard prize crews. The first was the *Alispa,* a vessel of about eighty tons burthen, laden with crockery and hardware; the second, a Mexican of similar size and loaded with an assorted cargo, was the *Telegraph.*

These vessels were manner by prize crews under command of Midshipman Robert Foster and sent into Matagorda to be condemned by order of district court and sold.

The Texas schooners continued up the Gulf. They

burned the Mexican schooner *Adventure;* they captured the schooner *Union,* flying a similar flag; they sank or burned numerous pirogues off Sisal, Telchac and Chuxenla—then came at last to Alacran.

The *Invincible* and the *Brutus* had scarce slipped into the roadstead off the Isle with two of their prizes in tow than the lookout on the *Invincible* descried a strange sail beating in from seaward.

Captain Thompson immediately hoisted the Mexican flag, hoping it would serve as decoy, but the stranger was wary. She hauled and shaped her course around a shoulder of the island, indicating that she was making a run for it.

Thompson, seizing his speaking trumpet, spoke the *Brutus.*

"Get under way," he order Captain Boylan. "Give her a chase."

The stranger, a well-trimmed schooner, had not yet shown her colors, and did not until the *Brutus,* breaking out the Star of the West, ran in close enough to give her two guns. The schooner then hauled her wind and hove to, at the same time running the English flag to her fore peak.

But the colors of Her Majesty's government held no terrors for Captain Boylan. He went aboard to examine the ship's papers.

She proved to be the English schooner *Eliza Russell,* 180 tons, laden with a general assortment of merchandise consigned to a Mexican merchant of Yucatan, J. G. Guiterrez.

The commanding officer, Captain Joseph Russell, was

indignant. He charged that the *Brutus* had committed an act of piracy and threatened to have the British Navy take a hand in the matter, but Captain Boylan replied that threats worried him not in the least; that since the *Eliza Russell* was carrying goods to the port of a nation at war with Texas, he considered her legitimate prey, and so he put a prize crew aboard and took the vessel back to the *Invincible*.

The two-ship fleet lifted anchors a few days later and headed for Texas—and, after capturing and stripping the Mexican schooners *Correo* and *Rafaelita* on the voyage in—arrived at Galveston bar on August 26th.

The *Brutus,* towing a prize, went in across the bar, but the *Invincible,* being of greater draft, elected to remain outside pending improved conditions—and the separation of the two ships spelt their doom.

Early next morning the crew of the *Brutus* was awakened by firing, and they looked across the bar to see two Mexican brigs hammering away at the *Invincible* with one broadside after another. The enemy ships, which had slipped up in the night, were the *Libertador* and that same *Vencedor del Alamo* which the *Invincible* had once chased into Vera Cruz.

After all these months she was answering with a vengeance the challenge she had received from Captain Jere Brown.

The *Brutus* immediately put about to go to her sister ship's relief, but in his haste to reach the scene Captain Boylan ran her on the bar, where she stuck fast.

Meanwhile, the *Invincible,* single-handed, was carrying the fight as best she could. It was close work, and the thunder of the guns, rolling in over the Gulf, brought out the town of Galveston to watch the uneven contest. On the shore the citizens, unable to help in any way, watched first the *Vencedor* and then the *Libertador* slip up to fire a broadside into the Texan, then turn and come back for another.

The *Invincible* was gallant. She fought back 'till her guns were hot and then, unable to withstand the pounding any longer, Thompson decided to risk her to the bar in the hope of gaining the safety of the harbor. He turned the scarred and battered schooner and made for the bar, and at first, it appeared to those who watched from the shore, that she would make it—then she scraped and struck.

The crew went overboard as the two Mexicans fired a final salvo and then stood off.

In the night the *Invincible,* a gallant craft while she lasted, went to pieces.

In the morning she was scratched from the navy list.

Thompson failed to get another command—but not because he had lost the *Invincible*. He had scarcely stepped ashore before the crew began making charges against him, complaints based largely on alleged cruelty to the men under his command.

Lieutenant Oscar Davis complained that the skipper was continually saying to him: "Goddamn you, sir, why don't you do this, and why don't you do that."

And there were other charges.

Today, in the State Archives at Austin, may be found the handwritten depositions of the crew. One claimed that Thompson, when a prize crew had requested fresh drinking water, had replied: "Drink the water alongside." Another said that the captain used the bottle more than was good for him, and often was asleep on deck in sight of the enemy; and still another charged that "in the capture of the brig *Correo* he appropriated to his own use six pair of pantaloons and fourteen shirts."

The Navy Department was after Thompson, too, but not Secretary Fisher—for Fisher was no longer secretary, President Houston having asked his resignation because he had left his office to go on the cruise.

The Department sent Thompson a series of questions dealing with incidents of his voyage, and in making his reply he reiterated those questions and followed them with answers. Following are a few samples:

"Why did I burn their towns?"

"A. Because they fired upon our flag when we were peacefully going ashore to replenish our water."

"Why did I demand contribution at Sisal?"

"A. My being on the enemy's coast and having prisoners on board eating our provisions, I wished to land them under a flag of truce, having taken their parole that none of them would take up arms against the Republic of Texas. I stated (at the time of landing the prisoners) in a communication to the commanding officer at the Castle, that I had sufficient force to take their town, and requesting him to remove to some place of safety the women and children and the old and decrepit persons, as I intended bombarding the town unless they paid to the government of Texas the small sum of $25,000, in consideration of which I should guarantee they would not be molested for a period of six months; the first reply to which was a twenty-four pound shot close under our main chains, our white flag still flying at the fore. This want of respect to our flag of truce induced me to open our broadsides on the town and castle, and the action became general, lasting three hours and thirty minutes, we receiving no damage."

The government intimated that it was quite all right to bombard Sisal and worry the Mexicans about contributions—but what right did Thompson have to promise immunity from shot for six months? The Republic didn't like, either, his methods of handling the crew, so Thompson was suspended. He died before being brought to trial.

President Sam Houston had released the schooner *Eliza Russell*, because he wanted to keep England friendly to the infant Republic. Great Britain hadn't been very pleased over that incident, and there were hints that the Royal Navy might help raise some of the future thunder on the Gulf.

That phase of the situation is explained in the following item carried by the Houston Telegraph, a story which also reveals the pride and confidence the people of Texas placed in their tiny sea force:

"We learn from the New Orleans Picayune that the English government has instructed her naval commanders to treat the Texian navy as pirates. We suspect this is a hoax, but if true we care not, for the stern lesson of 1776 has taught us that the mere dictum of Great Britain cannot make a whole people pirates or rebels. Let another England listen to that voice of experience, which has once thundered in her deaf ear the startling fact that *such* pirates *may become* formidable even to the British lion.

"The British vessel which was captured by our navy was a lawful prize; she had enemy's property on board and was without the limits of the neutral jurisdiction. Her cargo, therefore, would have been condemned in a prize court, according to a clear and well settled principle of the law of nations; a principle which Great Britain has herself sustained against the united powers of Europe. Our Executive, although aware of this fact, released the *Eliza Russell,* not through fear, but because he wished that Texas while in her infancy should adopt that precept, which is most in accordance with republican principles, and which the United States has so long and so nobly labored to sustain, viz: That neutral ships make neutral goods."

CHAPTER VI

THE INDEPENDENCE STRIKES HER COLORS

The *Independence,* flagship of the Texas Navy, rolled in an easy sea; and for this Captain George Wheelwright, her commander, thanked those gods who guide the destinies of mariners.

Ill luck had been with him in New Orleans, where he had been on a recruiting mission. Of the crew he had managed to muster, thirty-one men and boys, only six of the lot were seamen enough to know one part of a ship from another. Of course, the officers were seasoned, but it requires more than officers to sail a schooner, even on glassy water.

On the evening of April 10, 1837, the *Independence* had lifted anchor at New Orleans and had slipped down the Mississippi, bound for the Texas port of Velasco. She carried a few passengers, among them William H. Wharton, the Republic's minister to the United States, who was returning home from Washington.

At 5:30 o'clock on the morning of April 17th the slow sailing *Independence* was in latitude 29 degrees North, longitude 95 degrees and 20 minutes West, wallowing along off the Texas coast. A gray mist hung low over the sea, but that did not prevent the sharp eyes of the lookout from detecting two tall ships, with all sail set, bearing down on the schooner.

They were about six miles to windward, and they flew no colors, but the lookout was taking no chances.

"Look like Mexicans," he informed Lieutenant J. W. Taylor, who chanced to be officer of the deck at the time.

"Man the guns and clear for action!" he ordered.

Captain Wheelwright came on deck to take command. Knowing as he did what landlubbers he had shipped at New Orleans, his face wore a frown of worry. He gave hurried instructions to his lieutenants—Mr. Taylor, J. T. K. Lothrop, W. P. Bradburn and Robert Cassin.

"Scatter the experienced men among the guns, Mr. Taylor," said the captain. "And you, Mr. Bradburn, see that she's kept on the course for Velasco."

The *Independence* mounted but seven guns, half a dozen six-pounders and one long nine; and Gunner George Marion already was standing by the carriage of the nine.

Surgeon Levy stood a little apart; his work would come later. William Wharton had joined the captain, and they watched together as the tall ships edged down, one in the wake, the other on the weather quarter.

"Hoist the colors!" ordered Wheelwright—and the Texas Star fluttered up to the peak.

The two brigs answered immediately—with the flag of Mexico—but even that identification wasn't necessary now, as the two vessels were quite close enough to be recognized as the *Vencedor del Alamo* and the

Libertador, the first mounting sixteen medium eighteen-pounders, the latter eight brass twelves and a long eighteen.

It was now 9:30 a. m., and the *Vencedor del Alamo* moved up in the Texan's wake preparatory to raking her, the *Libertador* continuing to move in on the weather quarter.

At a distance of less than a mile she let go a broadside from her starboard batteries, the *Independence* returning the fire from her weather battery, consisting of three sixes, the pivot and the long nine-pounder.

"Hold your fire for closer quarters!" sang out Captain Wheelwright. "But keep the fuses ready."

The weather now freshened, and the *Independence,* still attempting to run for Velasco, heeled over until her lee guns were almost continually under water, with even the weather ones occasionally dipping their muzzles.

But the Texan's crew which, remember, numbered but six experienced seamen, now opened action, firing one broadside after another.

The *Vencedor* still crept up in the wake, and the cannonading remained brisk on both sides for nearly two hours.

Then the *Libertador,* still holding to the weather quarter, bore away and run down to within two cable lengths of the *Independence,* luffed and let go a broadside of round shot, grape and canister . . . the brig *Vencedor* continuing her raking from the wake.

But the landlubbers aboard the Texas ship were getting in some damaging shots. One ball took away the *Libertador's* main top-gallant mast, another unshipped one of her gun carriages, and a third took a chip off the after part of the foremast. It fell and killed two men as sails and rigging crumpled to the deck. One spar narrowly missed Commodore Lopez of the Mexican Navy, who was aboard with Captain Davis.

After fifteen minutes of hot action, the *Libertador* hauled her wind and widened her distance, then opened fire once more.

At 11 a. m. the Mexican again bore away, ran close in to the *Independence's* quarter and broke another broadside of round shot, grape and canister, which took down some of the Texan's rigging. She then returned to her former position and played out round shot, one of which went through the Texan's hull.

At 11:30 another ball passed through the quarter gallery of the *Independence,* and the ship sustained its first casualty—Captain Wheelwright himself. The ball knocked the speaking trumpet from the hand of the skipper, who was leaning against the gallery shouting orders.

He was sent below with three mangled fingers and a severe wound in his right side. He left the command to Lieutenant Taylor.

The three ships continued on their respective courses and positions, keeping up an incessant fire for full thirty minutes.

The *Vencedor* luffed and gained on the *Independence's* weather quarter; the *Libertador* at the same time bearing away and running down on the Texan's stern within easy pistol shot to put a broadside over the exposed decks of her enemy.

The *Vencedor* moved up with her raking fire and Wheelwright, seeing that further resistance was useless, sent word up to Taylor to surrender.

The Texas flag came down in the face of the enemy —for the first and only time in the history of the Texas Navy.

Captain Davis, commander of the Mexican brig *Libertador* sent word that he was ready to receive Taylor aboard, and though the Lieutenant complied, he did not give up his sword.

"I am your prisoner," he told Captain Davis, "but my sword you shall never receive."

He unsheathed it, walked to the rail, and threw it overboard.

The good people of Velasco, who had witnessed the final stages of the battle and its unhappy ending, watched helplessly as the two Mexican brigs started for Brazos Santiago with their prisoners aboard the *Independence,* which was in tow.

In Brazos Santiago there was great rejoicing, but Commodore Lopez and his subordinates treated the prisoners . . . including Wharton, the minister to the United States . . . with the greatest civility. Even Thomas M. "Mexico" Thompson, whose *Correo Mexicana* was captured by the Velascons in 1835 and who later was captured aboard the brig *Pocket,* was there. Having at last won back to Mexico, he now skippered the new *Bravo.*

But "Mexico" Thompson, the British adventurer,

harbored no animosities again the Texans. Wharton and some of the officers were exchanged after several months, and Thompson helped Captain Wheelright and several others escape—going with them to join the Texas Navy at Galveston, where in time he was appointed a post-captain at the Navy Yard maintained there.

The capture of the *Independence* pre-dated only by a short time the loss of the *Brutus* and the *Invincible* on Galveston bar. The *Liberty* already had been sold for debt in New Orleans. With the exception of one small boat, the receiving ship *Potomac,* the first official Texas Navy had passed into oblivion.

A few privateers still held Letters of Marque and Reprisal but the Texas Republic was attempting to recall these . . . because, one suspects, the government was not getting its twenty per cent out of the loot.

But Texas had to have a navy. Soon there would be new sail and new hulls . . . greater and grander ships to be sent prowling, like sea wolves, down the Mexican Main.

Chapter VII

NEW SAIL AND NEW HULLS

On the morning of May 22, 1839 the Galveston shore batteries thundered a salute of twenty-one guns as the pilot boat breasted the bar on her way in from three foreign ships which lay in the outer roadstead.

The pilot was bringing a distinguished visitor, an alert little man whose blue tunic, trimmed with the stripes of high rank, had also an empty right sleeve.

He was Charles Baudin, Admiral of the French Navy; and as he landed with his officers at the wharf the assembled citizens of Galveston went wild with acclaim. Everybody knew the significance of that empty sleeve—knew that the Admiral's right arm had been carried away by a British ball at the Battle of Trafalgar—but the Texas reception was in recognition of quite another event.

Baudin, on the flag frigate *Neriad,* and accompanied by the brig *Curossier* and the steamer *Phaeton,* had just arrived from Mexico where—by special act of Providence—he had been keeping the Mexican fleet busy at a time when Texas had no ships to put upon the Gulf.

Late in 1838 the French, having certain claims on Mexico, had blockaded the eastern ports, and at 2 p.m. on November 27 Baudin had attacked the fortress of San Juan d'Ulloa, the gateway to Vera Cruz; and although the fortress was defended by 160 pieces of artillery and four thousand men, it capitulated after several hours bombardment with a loss of five hundred. Baudin, after destroying several ships of the Mexican Navy, had entered Vera Cruz.

Santa Anna, at the head of a brigade of cavalry, made one attempt to recapture the city and, coming closer to the enemy than he intended, had a leg shot off by the efficient French gunners . . . which episode made Admiral Baudin doubly a hero in the estimation of admiring Galveston.

There is little doubt that the French, in those perilous days of 1838 and 1839, helped keep the course of Texas history on its even way. The first Texas Navy was out of commission—the *Liberty* sold for debt, the *Invincible* and the *Brutus* wrecked, the *Independence* a prize. With only one craft left, the leaky receiving brig *Potomac,* the entire Texas coast would have been open to invasion but for the French fleet keeping the enemy engaged.

Meanwhile, President Mirabeau B. Lamar and other officials of the Texas Republic were frantically making plans for the creation of a new sea force. In the shipping center of Baltimore the Texas commissioner to the United States, Samuel Williams, was busy. He recommended, first, that in the interest of safety the Texas government purchase the steamer *Charleston* at a price of $120,000 and arm her for coast defense duty.

The Texas Congress acted at once and the *Charles-*

ton, rechristened the *Zavala* and equipped with eight guns, became the nucleus for the second navy.

The next month, November 1838, Williams placed with Frederick Dawson, Baltimore ship builder, a rush order for one ship, two brigs and three schooners at a cost of approximately $800,000, including armament. John G. Tod, a former officer in the United States Navy, was sent from Texas to Baltimore, to see that the job was properly done.

The *Zavala* arrived at Galveston in March, 1839, and then one by one, at intervals of a month or two, the contract vessels began sliding down the ways. Fortunately, at this time the Mexican navy, weakened by the French attacks and faced with the insurrection which had been brewing in Yucatan, had trouble enough at home—giving Texas ample opportunity to equip and officer her new navy.

Thus, the early months of 1840 found the four-year-old Republic boasting a neat little fleet headed by the Sloop-of-War Austin, a 600-ton vessel carrying twenty medium twenty-four pound guns.

There were three armed schooners, the *San Jacinto,* the *San Bernard* and the *San Antonio,* each of 170 tons and carrying five guns; and besides the eight-gun *Zavala* and the receiving brig *Potomac* there were several smaller vessels like the *Colorado* (later the *Archer*), which were never destined to play major roles in Texian naval history.

The *Austin,* being the largest of the fleet, was designated as flagship, and since the officers of the old navy automatically had been retired with the breakup of the fleet, the Republic placed a new commander on her quarter-deck.

His name was Edwin Ward Moore, and he was only thirty years of age. Born at Alexandria, Virginia in June of 1810, Edwin Moore had entered Annapolis early in 1825 at the age of fourteen.

After graduation from the Academy he served as a midshipman on the *U. S. S. Hornet* of the West India Squadron; and then, in the same rank, he had transferred to the *Fairfield*, which was doing Mediterranean service. Promoted to lieutenant's rank in March of 1835, he later cruised in Mexican Gulf water aboard the U. S. Sloop-of-War *Boston*, and it was on this tour of duty that he caught the Texas spirit.

He impressed those Texan officials with whom he came in contact during calls at south coast ports, and since these officials had a weather eye out for a young and capable commander for the new navy, they offered Moore the job—with the rank of Post-Captain at a monthly salary of $200.

The voice of Adventure whispered in the ear of the blue-eyed, brown-haired, stocky sailor. He resigned his commission in the United States Navy and took over the sea forces of the infant Republic.

When he first assumed command Moore had only the *Zavala* and the practically worthless receiving ship, but even before the new vessels began arriving at Galveston navy yard the new Post-Captain . . . who also carried the honorary title of Commodore . . . had been recruiting.

The *Zavala*, the *Austin*, the *San Antonio* and the

others went one by one to New Orleans to tie up in the river while ship officers searched the waterfront for adventurous tars who were willing to go aboard for seven dollars a month as marine privates, or twelve a month as seamen. Of course, the pay scale ran higher for the qualified grades. Lieutenants and surgeons received $100, boatswains $40, midshipman $25, petty officers $19, marine lieutenants $30, sergeants $15, and corporals $9.

On Dauphine and Chartres and on other Vieux Carre streets where sailors seek rest from the sea, Commodore Moore and his lieutenants found their men, including a few gunners late from Her Britannic Majesty's navy . . . and with this salty assemblage in the fo'castle the second Texas Navy soon was ready to shot her guns and spread her sails to raise a new peal of thunder on the Gulf.

And just in time, for trouble was brewing in the south. Mexico had proclaimed a blockade for Texas ports. Yucatan, under the leadership of its new governor, Don Santiago Mendez, was in open revolt against the Central Government of Mexico. The Mexican government had ordered new ships of war from Europe and the States.

President Lamar of Texas had been sizing up the situation. The Mexicans, undoubtedly, would make short work of the Yucatecos, and the latter's comic-opera navy of one brig and two small schooners. What then? Well, it seemed reasonable to assume that once the internal strife had been settled, Mexico then could launch her long-delayed invasion of Texas.

What better then, reasoned Mirabeau Lamar, than to send the Texas Navy south to lend the Yucatecos a helping hand, and perhaps form an unofficial alliance which would distract the enemy from the Texas coast? At least some sort of diplomatic relations could be established, and that might be helpful if, and when, Yucatan won her independence.

At Galveston the Texas flotilla swung at anchor, awaiting orders. The flagship, in addition to Commodore Moore, was officered by Lieutenants E. P. Kennedy, D. H. Crisp, J. H. Baker and William Seegar. Aboard the *Zavala* with Captain J. T. K. Lothrop were Lieutenants George Henderson, and W. C. Brashear. The *San Bernard* was commanded by Lieutenant W. S. Williamson, who had with him Lieutenants George W. Estes and W. A. Tennison.

The *San Jacinto* was in charge of Lieutenant W. R. Postell, whose aides were Lieutenants J. O. Shaughnessey and A. G. Gray. Lieutenant Alex Moore had command of the *San Antonio,* with Thomas Wood and A. J. Lewis his lieutenants. Captain George Wheelwright was on the quarter-deck of the brig *Wharton,* and J. Clark commanded the *Archer,* once the *Colorado.*

On June 24, 1840 orders arrived, and the flotilla, with the exception of the *Wharton* and the *Archer*—which were to remain for coast protection—weighed anchor and slowly moved out to open sea.

The *Austin,* bearing the broad pennant of Commodore Moore, led the way. Ere it left Bolivar Point behind it answered the salute of the shore batteries . . . whose gunners did not suspect they were acclaiming a sailor who would one day be called "the Nelson of Texas."

They only knew that the single Star of the West floated again on the Gulf of Mexico, and that new sail and new hulls plowed down the Main—to Yucatan.

Chapter VIII

OFF YUCATAN

At sea, outside Galveston, Commodore Moore opened his sealed orders. He would proceed, according to instructions, to Campeche and there contact, as soon as possible, Governor Santiago Mendez or General Anaya, leaders in the Yucateco revolt against the centralized Mexican government. He would ascertain from them the true feeling of the Yucatan insurrectos for the Republic of Texas.

The Texas squadron, spoiling for a fight, loafed down the Gulf of Mexico.

It put in at the Arcos Islands, touched at Sisal under the English colors, and in good time stood off Campeche, where the Commodore hoisted the Single Star of Texas and waited for a signal from shore.

Almost at once a five-gun schooner-of-war put out and came alongside the flagship *Austin*. It carried General Anaya and suite who came aboard to greet the commodore and extend to him the welcome of Yucatan. Proper arrangements were made, and the next day Moore conferred with Governor Mendez, who assured him that the ports of Yacatan always would be open to any Texian vessel that might sail that way.

Thus were welded the first bonds of Yucateco-Texan friendship which, at a later date, were to be made even stronger in the powder smoke and gunfire of combat against a mutual enemy.

With civilities exchanged and friendships cemented, the *Austin* and its consorts filled away and went scouting, hoping to pick up an enemy schooner or brig and pick a fight. The squadron scattered, and on August 20, 1840 the *Austin* met and spoke Her Britannic Majesty's Brig *Penguin,* enroute from Vera Cruz to Tampico in search of a pirate rumored to be operating in those waters. The master of the *Penguin* said that only a few days before he had encountered the *San Jacinto* and he left the impression with Moore that he had been quite pleased at the manner in which Lieutenant Postell had stood down for him before recognizing the *Penguin* as an Englishman.

From the brig Moore learned that the Mexican Centralists had no vessel of war in Vera Cruz, and so he sailed up within three miles of the harbor fortress, surveyed the shipping, and then put to sea to join the *San Jacinto* and later the *Zavala.*

The 1840 cruise of the Texian Navy might be called a routine duty tour except for two outstanding events —the wreck of the *San Jacinto* in November, and the bloodless capture of Tobasco in December.

Although the flotilla fought no engagements worthy of note certain log books from the fleet—still preserved in the archives of Texas University and the state library at Austin—contain all that salty flavour which goes with the sea and those who ride upon her breast.

On October 31 the *San Bernard* and the *San Jacinto* were lying off the Arcas Islands, the latter riding on one anchor. A storm blew up, the anchor chain slipped, and the *San Jacinto* was driven ashore, a total loss. The events which followed are described in the journal of Alfred Walke, a midshipman aboard that vessel:

"Oct. 31.—At 1:50 her stern struck. Hailed the *San Bernard* for assistance. At 2 obtained a boat and finding we could do no more all hands left the vessel, with all valuable instruments, signals, etc.

"Sunday, Nov. 1.—These twenty-four hours clear weather and rough sea. Employed in getting the provisions, spars and everything that could be moved, to the *San Bernard*. Made a raft to get the guns out. Sent the sick ashore under charge of Mr. Oliver and Mr. Dorsey.

"Monday, Nov. 2.—At daylight went on board the wreck and commenced sending things on board the *San Bernard* and getting everything ready to get the guns and sails out. At 8:30 got the long gun out and sent it alongside the *San Bernard*. At 9 a strange sail hove in sight, which proved to be the ship *Austin*. Got the starboard anchor and found the shank had parted. Got most of the water casks out of the hold. At 2 Lieutenant William Jon left in the boat for the ship and returned at 8 p. m.

"Thursday, Nov. 5.—Warped her up and beached her on the island.

"Friday, Nov. 6.—Crew employed in collecting things belonging to the vessel and in rigging tents ashore. *San Bernard* sailed. Seven were sent on *Austin*, which sailed at 8 o'clock."

Commodore Moore evidently went in search of the

Zavala to bring her to the scene, leaving Midshipman Walke and a detail to save parts of the wreck, which Walke says went to pieces on November 25. A continuance of the diary shows that the lads must have had a rather enjoyable stay on the island:

"Friday, Dec. 25.—Spent this day very pleasantly indeed, quite a paradise on the dear Arcas. I shall never forget it. At 3 o'clock set down o'er a kid of very good egg-nog—drank all my absent friends health and retired at 10:30 in a perfect state of happiness. Hurrah for the Arcas."

The *Austin* and the *Zavala* later returned for the men and the property salvaged, but in the meantime the two Texian men-o'-war had carried out a coup that was not only gratifying, but highly profitable. With the *Austin* in tow the steamer *Zavala* had boldly puffed up the San Juan Baptista river to Tobasco, then being held by Centralist troops.

The soldiers, hearing that the ships were coming, evacuated the town, and when Commodore Moore arrived he found his work easy. He delivered a simple ultimatum:

"Hand over $25,000 or we'll bombard Tobasco off the map!"

That was all—and as the *jefes* of Tobasco appraised the starboard batteries of the *Austin* they decided that it might be best to capitulate. They sent the money aboard—silver in heavy bags.

Commodore Moore distributed a portion of the loot among the officers and crew as prize money, then sailed back down the river. Later, reporting to Secretary of

Navy Louis P. Cooke on the Tobasco affair, he wrote:

"Levied a contribution of $25,000 with which supplies were obtained from New Orleans to enable the squadron to keep at sea upwards of ten months. . . . Had no shot fired at us as we were leaving."

Although Moore was not fortunate enough, on this cruise, to get a contest with the enemy at sea, he did have other luck, for in the same report he says:

"During this cruise one Mexican schooner was captured within five miles of Vera Cruz, sent to Galveston, condemned and sold for seven thousand dollars."

But even without fights there were casualties—the journal of Midshipman J. L. Mabry noting that Gunner James Garrett of the *Austin* died of the scurvy; that Seaman S. O. Sawyer fell overboard from the top gallant yard and was lost; that Seaman James Duffries and Steward Samuel Edgerton died of yellow fever.

The *San Bernard,* having been previously dispatched to Galveston with reports, the *Austin* and the *Zavala* called at Arcos Island on January 13, 1841, picked up the *San Jacinto* crew members left there, and on the 18th set a course for Texas. Midshipman Walke was taken aboard the flagship, and his log-book, now styled "Journal of the Texas Ship-of-War Austin, bearing the Broad Pennant of Commodore E. W. Moore," continues:

"Friday, Feb. 4, 1841—Got the first cutter from the navy yard (at Galveston). Sent all the sick on board the brig *Wharton*. Sent two spars and standing rigging of the *San Jacinto* to the navy yard. Crew employed unbending sails and unreeving running riggings.

"Saturday, Feb. 27.—Lieutenant Cummings left the ship for Velasco for deserters, taking with him R. Hughes.

"Sunday, Feb. 28.—Silvanus Scott departed this life.

"Tuesday, March 2.—At sunrise fired a salute of twenty-one guns in celebration of the fifth anniversary of the Independence of Texas. At Meridian repeated the salute of twenty-one guns in honor of the Independence of Texas.

"Wednesday, March 3.—At sundown fired a salute of twenty-one guns in honor of the Independence of Texas.

"Saturday, March 13.—Francis Stephenson kicked the bucket.

"Sunday, March 14.—At 2 sent the bodies of Francis Stephenson and James Riley on shore to be buried. Sent on shore seven sick men to remain. At 11:15 James Phillips kicked the bucket."

It would seem that the jolly tars of the Texian Navy could not tolerate inaction without getting into trouble. Desertions and attempts at desertion were frequent, and in connection with these and kindred crimes Commodore Moore made generous use of that scourging implement of punishment, the cat-o'-nine-tails—or, as the sailors of that day called it, "the cats."

Note these excerpts from Walke's journal:

"Sunday, May 16, 1841.—William Harris, Benjamin Hughes and James McCauley went ashore on liberty and deserted.

"Wednesday, May 19.—Mr. Grandy went ashore and deserted.

"Monday, May 17, 1841.—At 9:30 called all hands to witness punishment and punished William Adair and James Fairburst each with a dozen lashes with the cats and released William Simpson from irons.

"Monday, May 31.—Caught Chas. Morris, who deserted twelve months back, and brought him aboard and put him in irons.

"Tuesday, June 29.—At 10:30 a. m. called all hands to witness punishment and punished William Simpson, Charles Morris and William Adair with the cats. Took Collins out of irons. Discharged four men, their term of office having expired.

"Saturday, July 10.—At 10:20 a. m. called all hands to witness punishment and punished McElroy and Grass each two dozen with the cats for allowing men to attempt desertion, and the second cutter's crew one dozen each for assisting, and C. Collins for attempting to desert.

"Saturday, July 24.—Confined William Barrington (Commodore's steward) in irons for attempting to desert. Caught James, who deserted from the brig *Wharton,* and put him in irons. Crew employed in the rigging.

"Friday, July 30.—At 6 p. m. put John McCarty in double irons and gagged him for insolence and mutinous conduct.

"Saturday, July 31.—At 11 a. m. called all hands

to witness punishment and punished Barrington and McCarty each with two dozen with the cats, and gave James eighteen. Confined Barrington and McCarty in double irons again.

"Thursday, Aug. 12.—Punished Barrington with twelve lashes with the cats and released him, also released McCarty."

Commodore Moore evidently believed that by sparing the "cats" he would spoil the tars. The boys, it appears, merely wanted action; there would be plenty later on. . . .

Meanwhile the *San Bernard* had been on a cruise. President Lamar, in an attempt to obtain from Mexico recognition of Texas independence, had sent the schooner to Vera Cruz with Judge Webb, the minister designated to carry out negotiations, but Mexico rejected Webb's overtures and the *San Bernard* brought him back to Galveston on June 28.

In his report on this voyage Lieutenant D. H. Crisp, commanding, inserted a paragraph indicative of the Texas Navy's poverty at the time. Writing to the Commodore, he said:

'I found at Sacrificios (island off Vera Cruz harbor) Her Britannic Majesty's Sloop *Comus,* U. S. Sloop *Warren,* and Spanish Sloop *Le Altos.* I am sorry to say the poverty of this government, developed in my dress, prevented me from exchanging suitable civilities with the officers."

At the moment things were quiet in the south. Yucatan, still too weak for open conflict with the Mexican Centralists, was biding her time and shaping a policy.

Commodore Moore, on the *San Antonio,* was engaged in a charting expedition along the Texas coast —collecting data which would prove valuable enough for later publication by the U. S. government and the British Admiralty.

Mirabeau B. Lamar, the poet-president of the Texas Republic, was dreaming dreams, and hatching a personal plot which, when it took form, would again send the Texian Navy rolling down the Main.

Chapter IX

UNDER THE BROAD PENNANT

Mirabeau Buonaparte Lamar, the troubadour president of the Texas Republic, was ever a dreamer.

He wrote verse in his spare time and made songs of love while he went about the affairs of state, but in all his volumes of poesy can be found nothing half so romantic and intriguing as the verbal plot he hatched with the rebellious Yucatecos in the early days of July, 1841.

Texas, in those days, lived in continual fear of a new Mexican invasion, and Lamar . . . playing the lone-handed diplomat . . . reasoned that if the trouble center could be kept in Mexico's own backyard so much the better for the Republic; and Yucatan, contesting the power of the Centralist government, chanced to be that backyard for the moment.

Accordingly, in July, the poet-president dispatched a communication to the Yucateco governor, Don Santiago Mendez, proposing to confederate with him to render aid, and to receive reciprocal aid. Lamar offered the services of the Texas Navy, suggesting that Yucatan and Texas together might be able to worry the Centralists half out of their wits.

Don Santiago, as might be expected, was overjoyed, and he immediately sent a minister scurrying to Texas to complete negotiations.

This gentleman, Senor Martin Francisco Peraza, arrived on September 11 and within a few days he and Lamar reached an agreement—that Yucatan would pay Texas $8,000 for fitting out the fleet and $8,000 a month while the squadron remained in active service, the spoils from Mexican prizes to be divided. All this was agreed on without the consent or authority of the Texas Congress; it was, as Sam Houston later termed it, "a mere act of grace or will on the part of the President."

Lamar lost no time. He sent Lieutenant Lewis with messages to Commodore Moore, who was still on his coast survey with the *San Antonio* and the *San Bernard*. Moore, on receipt of orders, sailed at once for Galveston. There he received the down payment of $8,000 and he began outfitting.

On December 13, 1841, the vessels being ready, Commodore Moore hoisted the broad pennant and put to sea with sealed orders, the *San Antonio* and the *San Bernard* following in the *Austin's* wake.

Outside the bar the Commodore, in the presence of some of his officers, opened the orders. They were brief and to the point.

He would proceed to Sisal and then to the Yucatan capital of Merida. He would give all help possible to the Yucatecos.

He would stop Mexican ships and examine their cargoes for contraband. He would capture Mexican towns and levy contributions. He would destroy public works wherever possible. He would, in short, raise all the hell and thunder that he could along the eastern seaboard.

Guns shotted, the flotilla wallowed south, under full sail and a fair wind behind.

The work ahead was to Moore's liking, but he had one regret as he watched Bolivar Point fade astern—that he couldn't take the steamer *Zavala*. She was in need of repairs that the government could ill afford.

Early in January the *Austin* dropped her anchor off Sisal, and Commodore Moore learned that he had arrived just in time. The Yucatecos, despairing in their weakness, were about to sign a peace with Mexico, and conferences already were under way . . . but with the appearance of the 20-gun *Austin* and her consorts, the Yucatecos, after a mad and joyful celebration, changed their minds and decided on war.

Commodore Moore was quite the hero. Upon arrival he exchanged salutes with the castle and went ashore. Next day, in company with Lieutenant Commander William Seeger, he went to Merida to confer with the government and size up the situation. A short time later he sent the *San Antonio* to New Orleans for provisions, ordering her to touch at Galveston and leave his report to the secretary of navy. In it he said:

"If it be the wish of His Excellency the President (Sam Houston was executive now) to coerce Mexico to acknowledge our independence, I can at once blockade all the ports of entry, viz: Vera Cruz, Tampico and the Brazos de Santiago; and if I had the steamer *Zavala* to co-operate with the squadron I could levy contributions on several of their towns to a greater amount than the entire cost of the navy. . . . The vessels building in New York when I left Galveston, for the Mexican Navy, I will use my utmost to intercept, and if they have any contraband of War on board, I will send them to Galveston—this course being strictly in accordance with international law."

Moore concluded with the statement that he was leaving for Vera Cruz, off which place he expected to cruise for some time. He probably did not expect any serious engagements at sea, but he did intend to pick up any merchantmen he could find and keep a sharp lookout for the two Mexican war ships due from New York. The remainder of the Mexican navy was keeping close to port pending the arrival of these two vessels.

On a bright day in February a gay party was held aboard the British steamship *Solway,* lying in Vera Cruz harbor. A multitude of ladies and gentlemen, in gala attire, had come aboard to say farewells to friends who were about to leave in the steamer for Galveston.

Many of the guests stood at the *Solway's* rail watching the shipping in the harbor, but no vessel among the various nationalities attracted more attention than a tall, graceful warship which stood off the port entrance.

She carried at her peak the Stars and Stripes of the United States, and as she moved slowly up within cannon shot of San Juan d'Ulloa those on the *Solway* and other boats observed that she mounted about twenty guns. None, however, . . . not even the veteran skippers . . . could identify her.

The stranger did not approach the other shipping or come into port. After passing under the guns of the fortress, she swung about and stood off outside the harbor, like a great, restless bird with white wings.

Soon a rich Mexican merchantman, the *Priscosa,* put to sea bound for Tampico, and as she neared the strange ship a startling thing occurred.

The American flag went fluttering down, a gun boomed from the visitor's weather battery, and another flag went up the mast—the Single Star of Texas!

From the boats in the harbor a great shout went up—"The Texians! The Texians!"—and people ashore fled in all directions.

The *Priscosa* tried to run, but the warship fired another gun, then another and another. The cannon of San Juan were run out to the embrasures of the fort and great noise made, but the Mexican vessel struck her colors and was led off in glorious style by the stranger ship.

The Texans on the *Austin* took what cargo they needed from the merchantman and then went scouting for the two Mexican war schooners from New York, but on this score Moore was doomed to disappointment, as one vessel was wrecked on the way down and the other made it safely into Vera Cruz.

At noon of February 7 the *Austin,* cruising off Vera Cruz in company with the *San Bernard,* sighted a strange sail making for Sacrificios. The flagship immediately stood in chase and within an hour came up with the vessel, which proved to be the Mexican schooner *Progresso,* inbound from New Orleans.

Here was a legal prize and Moore, with his guns ready, hailed her and threatened a broadside unless she hove to. The *Progresso* complied at once and the Commodore ran up the Texas colors as he sent Lieutenant Gray to board the capture.

There was a general officer of the Mexican army on the schooner and as the Texas flag went up he tore his epaulettes from his shoulders and thrust them in his pocket, but Gray caught him in the act.

The *Progresso* proved to be a valuable prize, carrying as she did a cargo of flour and sugar. Moore made the crew prisoners—to be put ashore later at an isolated point—and then put a prize crew of his own aboard the schooner under command of Lieutenant William Tennison.

At six in the evening the *Progresso* filled away and stood for the northeast, bound for Galveston and condemnation.

It may seem strange that Commodore Moore was twice able to trick the fortress of San Juan but the following article, which appeared in the Houston Star of March 17, 1842, indicates as much:

"We learn from Mr. Van Ness that a day or two before he sailed from Vera Cruz, Commodore Moore's flagship appeared before the castle, which saluted the vessel, supposing it to be an American corvette. The best pilot in the harbor was sent out to guide him into port, but as soon as the pilot got aboard the *Austin,* the Texian flag was run up and the vessel sailed proudly away before the freshening breeze, towards Yucatan. The Mexican armed schooner and steamship were lying in the port of Vera Cruz, and scarcely a man was on board them. It is supposed that Moore intends to compel the pilot to guide him into port, and cut them out from under the guns of the castle. Success attends the brave."

What he did with the pilot is not a matter of record.

Arriving off Campeche in the first week of March, the Commodore received two surprising communications from Texas and New Orleans. First, he learned that there had been a mutiny aboard the *San Antonio* at New Orleans and that one of his best officers, Lieutenant Charles Fuller had been killed. Nine men had been involved and all had been jailed in the Crescent City. Moore evidently thought the mutineers were in irons aboard the *San Antonio,* which he expected to meet in a few days at Laguna, because he wrote to the navy department:

"I expect to meet Capt. Seeger at Laguna, for which place I leave tonight, and I will mete out to the rascals the uttermost penalties of the law."

How well he succeeded will be explained in a following chapter—for more than a year elapsed before the Commodore finally got his hands on the "rascals."

When the *Austin* contacted the *San Antonio* at *Laguna* the commander received his second shock. It came in the form of a presidential order directing him to return with the fleet to Galveston—and the order was dated December 15, 1841, just two days after Moore had left Galveston for Yucatan!

On the very day of the sailing Sam Houston had taken over the presidency from Mirabeau Lamar, and since the "Raven" had never favored Lamar's alliance with Yucatan, the order had been one of his first official acts, but it had been written too late to catch Moore.

Now, three months later, the Commodore received it . . . and ignored it. He considered that he had unfinished business in Mexican waters, and by remaining on cruise he opened a breach which was to make Sam Houston a lasting enemy.

Instead of going to Galveston the Commodore took the *Austin,* the *San Antonio* and the *San Bernard* to Vera Cruz, and the scope of his unfinished business in those waters is best explained by excerpts from a report he made to the department a month later.

"I discovered that the steamer under the castle was raising steam, and the schooner now under Mexican colors was warping alongside her," he wrote. "I immediately run up the boat and began making preparations to give them a warm reception, standing out to get an offing, the wind being very light, and we being barely out of gun-shot of the Castle. I remained near all day, passing once inside of one of the reefs forming the harbor, but they did not come out. . . . The following forenoon I captured the Mexican schooner *Doloritas* nine days from Matamoras bound to Vera Cruz. She was very near the land when we discovered her, and the supercargo and part of the crew made their escape in the boat. She parted company yesterday for Galveston, and in the afternoon I landed the Captain, Mate and boy with all their private effects at Point Delgada.

"On the 3rd inst., within a few miles of Tuspan, we captured the Mexican schooner *Dos Amigos,* from

Matamoras, bound for Tuspan with a cargo of salt. I will dispatch her also to Galveston tonight or tomorrow, in company with the *San Bernard*. ..."

During this cruise it appears that the tars of the three ships did a great deal of talking about the late mutiny aboard the *San Antonio,* and at one time Moore took precautions to prevent a similar outbreak on the flagship. This is noted in the logbook kept by Midshipman Edward Johns of the *Austin,* a journal now preserved in the archives at the University of Texas. It says:

"March 7, 1842—Removed all the small arms from the armory and storeroom to the wardroom, and put William Beatts in double irons for making use of mutinous and threatening language. At 8:30 called all hands to muster. Commodore Moore read the articles of war to them."

The Johns diary also reveals the zeal displayed by the Texans in quest of contraband shipping. These two entries, for instance:

"April 18.—From 4 to 8 light breezes and fine weather. At 5 made the land bearings, brailed up the spanker and wore ship. At 5 strange sail in sight on the weather bow, made chase. At 7 came up with her, hove to, lowered the boat and boarded her. She proved to be the Yucatan schooner. *Attevido* from Sisal bound to the eastward. At 7:30 filled away. At 8 the shipping as Sisal in sight ... at 10:20 came to anchor. At 10:50 piped down.

"April 20.—At anchor off Sisal. These 24 hours moderate breezes from the N&E and pleasant weather. A strange sail in sight standing towards us. At 4 p. m. strange sail hoisted Spanish colors. At 4:10 beat to quarters and cleared ship for action, Spanish frigate standing for us. At 6 she came to anchor on our larboard bow. Secured the guns and beat the retreat. Sent Lt. Gray to board her. At 7:45 Lt. Gray returned, the vessel proving to be the Spanish frigate *Isabella* from Havana."

On April 25 the squadron anchored off Campeche and Commodore Moore went ashore to collect $8,000 —the sum Yucatan owed as a month's rental for the Navy's services. Next day the three vessels were taking a course for Galveston.

Chapter X

THE MUTINY ON THE SAN ANTONIO

Seymour Oswald, sergeant of Marines aboard the Texian Schooner-of-War *San Antonio,* was a most unhappy man.

Several times during the past few months, in punishment for insubordination, he had been stripped to the waist, lashed to a cannon, and thoroughly whipped—and the bite of the terrible cat-o'-nine-tails was quite enough to make any man unhappy.

He had no love for any of his officers, and for all he cared the devil could take them—the Commodore; Commander Lothrop; Lieutenant Fuller; and particularly his own skipper, Captain William Seeger.

Sergeant Oswald sometimes thought of desertion, but after mulling it over and finding no hope of vengeance in such an act, he decided to wait for a better plan. And then, while the *San Antonio* and the *San Bernard* were taking on fresh water at the Isle of Mugeres, on the east tip of Yucatan, he became possessed of the Great Idea.

He conferred with Benjamin Pompilly, a seaman who also harbored grievances against authority, and the two put their heads together. They discussed whom they could trust and whom they couldn't, and then one day . . . while ashore with most of the crew filling the water casks . . . the plan for mutiny was broached.

Most of those who met on the beach were men who had felt the scourge of the "cats"—Captain of Marines William Simpson, Seaman Frederick Sheppard, James Hudgins, Isaac Allen, William Barrington, John Williams, and Marine Antonio Landois. Even Edward Keenan, the cook, was there.

Oswald it was who outlined the project.

"'Twill be easy, lads," he said, "but we've got to get some of the San Bernard men with us. We can slip a few muskets out of the wardroom, strike some night at a signal, and take the officers afore they know what we're about . . ."

"An' give them a taste o' the cats," suggested someone in the crowd.

"Maybe, but not so fast," cautioned the spokesman. "The plan is this . . . we must see some of the San Bernard men and make arrangements with them. Then, when we give the signal to strike, the lads of the Bernard will strike, too. We'll take both schooners, run 'em into Vera Cruz, and sell 'em to the Mexs."

With the exception of Frederick Sheppard, who was dubious about the whole affair, the plan met unanimous approval, and the conspirators, after swearing all to secrecy, adjourned for the purpose of feeling out the men of the *San Bernard*.

And there the matter ended, at least temporarily. As related in the preceding chapter, Commodore Moore sent the *San Antonio* to New Orleans for provisions, thus unwittingly frustrating the plans made on the Isle of Mugeres.

The *San Antonio* dropped anchor in the Mississippi

The Mutiny on the San Antonio

late on February 10, 1842 and next morning Captain Seeger went ashore to buy the supplies, leaving Lieutenant Charles Fuller in command, with orders to grant no shore liberties until his return.

Now the old city under the levee has ever been famed as a place where liquor flows easily and in large quantities; and the Texas tars, having been long at sea, thought fondly on the joys to be found in the grog shops along Dauphine. The rebellious group, after having obtained from some source enough liquor to whet their appetites for more, decided to go ashore.

Sergeant Oswald and Pumpilly took it upon themselves to force the issue and, accompanied by several other half-drunken members of the clique, they came aft and demanded of M. Dearborn, officer in charge of the deck, that they be given liberty permits.

"Back to your quarters!" snapped the officer. "The old man is ashore and there's no one on board authorized to grant liberty."

"Then we'll go anyhow," growled the sergeant. "What say, lads, are you with me?"

They answered that they were, and Mr. Dearborn advised them not to try it, whereupon the Marine continued to urge the point by use of language that fair blistered the spars, and which brought Lieutenant Fuller from below to see what the disturbance was about.

Sensing something serious in the air, Fuller gave an order: "Arm the Marine guard, Mr. Dearborn, and put these men under arrest!"

The order infuriated Oswald, who drew a tomahawk

from his belt and struck at the lieutenant, but missed.

Then Pumpilly drew a pistol. He fired once—and the Lieutenant dropped dead on the deck.

"That," said Pumpilly, "is for the dozen you gave me with the cats."

The melee now became general, the mutineers against the officers and a few loyal members of the crew. Antonio Landois had obtained a musket from some secret hiding place. He clubbed it and downed Midshipman Allen as the latter rushed into the fray with flying fists.

Landois then gave Midshipman Odell a nasty bayonet wound as Odell came to the rescue of Allen.

As none of the officers but the dead lieutenant had been armed the fight was soon over, the mutineers using their pistol and musket to force the officers aft and down into the cabin. Then they lowered a boat and attempted to escape, but the pistol shot which killed Fuller had been heard aboard the U. S. Revenue Cutter *Jackson,* which was standing nearby, and before the rebels could reach shore they were taken in custody by Captain Day of the cutter.

That night they sobered in the city jail, where they were to remain for a year before Commodore Moore found opportunity to "mete out to the rascals the uttermost penalties of the law."

Even at that their act of mutiny gave them a longer lease on life than that enjoyed by their shipmates, for the *San Antonio* was about to become the mystery ship of the Mexican Gulf.

Again, as explained in the preceding chapter, the

schooner returned to Yucatan to rejoin the *Austin* and the *San Bernard,* and with those two ships went up to Galveston in April.

There the officers and men read for the first time the proclamation of blockade which had been issued by President Sam Houston on March 29th. It read:

"To all to whom these presents shall come: Know ye, that I, Sam Houston, President of the Republic of Texas, and Commander-in-chief of the Army and Navy, by virtue of my authority, and the power vested in me by law, and for the purpose of more effectually prosecuting the war in which Texas is now engaged with Mexico, do hereby order, decree and proclaim, that all ports of the Republic of Mexico on its eastern coast, from Tobasco, in the state of Tobasco, to Matamoras, in the State of Tamaulipas, including those ports, and comprising the mouth of the Rio Grande del Norte, and the Brazos Santiago: and also, all the inlets, estauries and passes on the said eastern coast of Mexico—and, from and after the date of this proclamation, in a state of actual and absolute blockade, by the armed vessels of this nation.

"And for the purpose of carrying this order, decree and proclamation into complete effect, an armed naval force now is, and will be continued to be kept at or near the said ports and passes of the eastern coast of Mexico entirely sufficient to enforce this decree.

"For any breach or effort at breach of this blockade the offending vessel and cargo will be liable to confiscation, and the officers and mariners of such vessel will be subject to the penalties attached to a breach of blockade. This decree shall take effect as to vessels sailing from New Orleans within three days after its publication in that city, and within five days as to any neutral port within the Gulf of Mexico—within twenty days as to any port of the United States, north of the Gulf of Mexico—and in forty-five days as to vessels from any port in Europe.

"In witness whereof, I have hereunto affixed my hand and the Great Seal of the Republic, at the city of Houston, this 26th day of March in the year of our Lord, one thousand eight hundred and forty-two, and of the Independence of the Republic the seventh. Sam Houston."

In order to carry out this blockade the Texian fleet went to New Orleans to refit and prepare for sea, and in August the *San Antonio* was ready. She sailed first for Galveston, then for Matagorda, with orders to proceed to Yucatan; and as she hoisted sail for what was destined to be her last cruise Captain Seeger was warned that the crew was not all that it should be— that there were men aboard just as mutinous as those left in the New Orleans jail.

The Texian Schooner-of-War *San Antonio* dropped south from Galveston bar on August 27, 1842 with provisions for three months on board. She was never heard from again. . . .

What happened to the *San Antonio?* Was she lost in the heavy gales that swept the Gulf in September and October? Or was she, as many suspected, converted into a pirate flying the Skull and Cross-Bones? Who can say? Anyhow, rumors bearing out the latter supposition persisted as late as the Spring of 1843. I quote an article published in Nassau, New Providence, in March of that year:

"The U. S. Brig *Boxer* arrived here March 13 from a cruise. The *Boxer* fell in with a vessel near the Isle of Pines which answers the description of the *San Antonio*. The captain thinks it was her. The master says he is sure he has seen her at Galveston and does not think he can be mistaken. The first lieutenant thinks she was a slaver. She showed no colors. The *Boxer* first ran up a French flag, the signal not being returned, the American ensign was run up and a fire opened on the schooner, the captain hoping to disable her. He believes that only one shot told. The distance was near two miles when she was first discovered. The chase continued two days but the winds were too light for the *Boxer*."

In the following month the Boston Post observed:

"Several opinions have recently been expressed in the papers about the fate of the Texian Schooner-of-War *San Antonio*. Some suppose that she was the long, low black schooner which was chased by the U. S. Brig *Boxer,* and that she is now a pirate."

All these accounts the New Orleans Tropic branded as "cock and bull stories," with the comment that Captain Seeger, before going to sea, had said:

"If I fall in with the Mexican fleet I shall not run, but shall attack them, and before the fate of the little schooner is settled she shall tell a tale worthy of the cause and the Navy."

Was Seegar killed at sea, and was his ship taken over by a mutinous crew that raised the Skull and Cross-Bones to carry on an illicit business on the Gulf? The Tropic didn't think so; it merely believed that the craft was victim of storm—but, adding to current rumors, it did publish a story that two former sailors of the boat, being overtaken by drink on Dauphine Street, had stated that: "The *San Antonio* is in good hands and you'll be hearing of her from San Jago de Cuba."

Anyhow, a low, black schooner was frequently reported off Isle of Pines and the south coast of Cuba. Her Britannic Majesty's frigate *Illustrious* was sent in search of her, but the cruise was in vain. The *San Antonio* went down in naval chronicles among the many ghost ships that have sailed over the horizon never to return.

Evil days were about to fall upon the Texas Navy, because of a lack of money to carry out badly needed repairs. The steamer *Zavala,* long unused, was becoming a rotting wreck; the *Austin* was leaking; the *Wharton* required new fittings; and, to make matters worse, the *San Bernard,* in September was driven ashore by storm at Galveston.

Fortunately, however, the services of the fleet were not badly needed at sea during this time because President Houston, seeing new hope of obtaining Mexican recognition, had, at the request of European powers, lifted the blockade on Mexican ports.

This breather gave Texas time to raise money and refit her little navy, the rebellious Yucatecos meanwhile keeping the Mexican navy busy. Most of the needed repairs were effected by November of 1842, and on the fifth of that month the New Orleans Tropic published an analytical story comparing the strength of the Texas and Mexican sea forces. At this time the loss of the *San Antonio* had not yet been certified, and the Tropic included her in the Texas list, although, in reality, the Republic now had but two serviceable ships, the *San Bernard* being ashore. The article, which reflects the high regard New Orleans had for the Texas navy, follows:

"We stated yesterday, on good authority, that the war steamer *Montezuma* had been added to the Mexican squadron. This makes the Mexican force upon the Gulf altogether superior, in number and metal, to the navy of the Lone Star Republic; though actually inferior, we believe events will prove, in point of efficiency and power. The Texian squadron, at the present time, consists of four vessels, viz:—

"The Ship *Austin*, bearing the broad pennant of Commodore Moore, mounting eighteen 24-pounders and two 18-pounders.

"The *Brig Wharton*, Capt. J. K. Lothrop, sixteen 18-pounders.

"Schooner *San Antonio*, W. Seeger, command'g- seven 12-pounders.

"Schooner *San Bernard,* D. H. Crisp, Lieut.—seven 12-pounders.

"Every gun on the Texian vessels throws shot far superior to the celebrated Paixhan shot, in many particulars, and far more destructive. The Mexican squadron is as follows:

"The Steamer *Montezuma,* mounting two 68-pounders and eight 32-pounders, all Paixhan guns. (The Paixhans used a hollow shot which broke with shrapnel effect when they struck.)

"The *Steamer Guadaloupe,* two 68-pounders, Paixhan guns.

"The *old City of Dublin* (rechristened *Regenerador*) two 18-pounders.

"Schooner *Eagle,* one 32 and six 18-pounders, Paixhan guns.

"Brig *Yucateco,* twelve 18-pounders and two 12-pounders.

"Brig *Campecheano,* one 18-pounder and six 12-pounders.

"Schooner *Sisalanio,* one 9-pounder and two 6-pounders.

"Altogether the seven Mexican vessels mount 45 guns, the four Texian vessels 50 guns—the Mexicans, it will be seen, having greatly the advantage in weight of metal. The Texians, however, are vastly superior to their antagonists in several points. In the first place the principal officers of the Texian navy are all men of the highest capabilities. Commodore Moore, Capt. Lothrop and Capt. Seeger, would be an honor to the naval service of any country. They are men of great energy and undaunted courage, and will do all that mortal men can do for the honor and glory of the Single Star.

"Each of these officers, by natural capability, by education, and by experience is worth the whole squalid and Heaven-abandoned herd of Mexicans afloat on the Gulf. They received their principles and spirit from too noble a source to prove unfaithful to their trusts. The Texian vessels, moreover, are manned by seamen of a race in whose veins never flowed the blood of cowards. They are generally true samples of the genuine Yankee Tars who have made the naval history of the United States, a simple history of the most brilliant achievements ever witnessed upon the ocean.

"On the other hand, the Mexicans are sadly deficient in the right material for officers and seamen. By an arrival yesterday we learn that Don Francisco de Paula Lopez has been appointed commander-in-chief of the navy by Santa Anna, suspending Commodore Marin. Lopez is somewhat known in the United States. He was at Baltimore in 1836, superintending the building for the Mexican government of the two 16-ton brigs which were subsequently captured by the French.

"During the revolution in Mexico, Lopez held command of the navy, and previously was in the Spanish service. He is now an old man, particularly deficient in the qualities demanded by the station he occupies. At no time of life has he been distinguished for energy, decision or ability. Commodore Marin, late in command of the Mexican squadron, is a very capable man, and if he is retained in the service the Mexicans have one decent officer. He is a Mexican by birth, and was midshipman in the Mexican navy under Commodore Porter.

"Captain Charleywood, having command of the steamer *Guadaloupe,* is said to be a good officer. By express stipulation his vessel is entirely under his own control, and he has a right to fight in his own way. Even Commodore Lopez can exercise no authority over him. The balance of the officers and men are made up up of Englishmen, Frenchmen, Italians, Mexicans, and a few Americans. According to all accounts they are in a sad state of insubordination, and lacking in all the essential requisites of good seamen. Such a crowd stands no chance against the perfect discipline of the Texian navy. In an action, they will probably injure each other about as much as they are injured by the enemy."

There was a great deal of prophecy in the Tropic's summary. The test was coming. . . .

Thomas F. McKinney who commanded the San Felipe in the contest with the *Correo Mexicano*.

The boys take a swim. A sketch from the journal of midshipman, Edward Johns of the flagship, Austin.

The application of Robert Potter, provisional secretary of the Navy, for a Letter of Marque—so that he might outfit a ship and "Cruise on the coast of the enemy." From the Navy papers in the Texas State Archives.

Sketches made by Edward Johns, Midshipman, on one of the covers of the journal he kept while at sea on the flagship Austin. The logbook is preserved in the University of Texas Archives.

Inventory and appraisement of the cargo on board the Schooner "Ana Maria" taken as a prize by the Schooner of War "San Antonio" and condemned to be sold by Judge A B Shelby. Sale to be made by the prize Agent, William J Bramham Esqr. Appraisement made by J Edmunds, James M Seymour, and William S Branum Esqrs commissioners appointed by the said Judge. Galveston November 23rd 1840.

301 sacks of flour averaging 20 lb ea	at pr sack	$5 ct	1,505 00
121 " Coffee " 210 lbs ea	25,200	10¢	2,520 00
8 Bales of plaintd flannels 96 pc	2784 yds	30¢	835 20
1 " samples of the above (no value)			
2 Bls Spirits Turpentine 32½ Gal ea	65 gls	50¢	32 50
1 sack Rice	100 lb		4 00
½ Barrel bread			1 50
3 small parcels coil rope			3 00
20 lb Old copper		12¢	2 40
4 gall Lamp Oil		125¢	6 00
1 Keg black paint			3 00
½ Cords Wood		$16	9 00
1 Schooner called "Ana Maria" of about 80 tons with all her tackle and apparel			858 00
	Total amt		$5,770 60

Galveston November 23rd 1840

We certify that the above is a true Inventory and appraisement of the prize Schooner "Ana Maria" together with her cargo, to the best of our knowledge and belief.

J Edmunds
Jas M Seymour } Commissioners
Wm S Branum

Partial list of goods taken from the "Anna Maria," a Mexican Merchantman seized as a prize by Texas Schooner-of-War, San Antonio. From Navy documents in Texas State Archives.

TEXIAN LOAN.

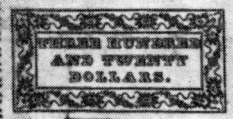

THREE HUNDRED AND TWENTY DOLLARS.

CERTIFICATE No.

Received, of THREE HUNDRED AND TWENTY DOLLARS, *being a Loan to the Government of Texas, for* FIVE YEARS, *at the rate of* EIGHT PER CENTUM PER ANNUM *Interest, payable annually at the Office of* WILLIAM CHRISTY, NOTARY PUBLIC, *in the City of* New-Orleans. *For the above amount, Land in Texas may be taken at the rate of* FIFTY CENTS *per Acre, upon the conditions and with the guarantees contained in a Contract executed this day at the Office of the said Christy, by the undersigned Commissioners and the said Lender.*

In Testimony Whereof, *we have hereunto set our hands, and affixed our seals, in the said City of* NEW-ORLEANS, *this Eighteenth day of January, one thousand eight hundred and thirty-six.*

L.S.
L.S.
L.S.

COMMISSIONERS ON THE PART OF TEXAS.

GOVERNMENT OF TEXAS.

SIX HUNDRED AND FORTY ACRES OF LAND.

Printed by Benjamin Levy—New-Orleans.

Commodore Edwin Ward Moore, Republic of Texas Navy. Drawn by J. Tom Jones from an original portrait, by courtesy of Mr. Eugene Moore Cochran.

contrary to an express act of Congress, but the manner, (<u>dishonorably discharged</u>,) is literally disfranchising the undersigned, directly in opposition to the Constitution; to preserve and maintain which, he claims to have made some sacrifices. He therefore respectfully asks that your Honble. body may direct a rigid examination into his conduct in order that he may if innocent enjoy the common rights of a freeman, and if guilty of any of the charges preferred against him, he does not expect or desire that the uttermost penalties of the laws which it is alleged he set at defiance or disregarded, will not be enforced upon his person—

In order that the Honble. Congress may understand clearly the difficulties that the undersigned has had to encounter in sustaining the Navy of Texas from 15 Decr. 1841 to 25 July 1843, he herewith transmits a printed address, and begs leave to state that he is prepared to produce the originals of the communications referred to in the same—

All of which is respectfully submitted to the Honble Congress for their appropriate action;

Your fellow citizen
E. W. Moore.

Washington
11 Jany. 1844.

A part of Moore's letter to Congress—demanding trial on President Houston's various charges against the Commodore. From Navy documents in State Archives at Austin.

Re-cast Texas Navy buttons, made from the original dies developed in the 1830's by Scovill Mfg. Co.

Chapter XI

PIRATES ALL!

When Samuel Houston, president of the Republic of Texas, grew angry his wrath was no light and passing thing—and he was harboring a particularly venomous wrath in the early days of January, 1843.

All because of the two-ship Texas Navy. It wasn't, in the opinion of the chief executive, earning half its beef and grog; and was costing, altogether, much more than the infant nation could afford.

But that wasn't the seat of the anger which surged in the breast of the Raven. Repeatedly he had ordered the *Austin* and the *Wharton* home to Galveston navy yard—and they hadn't come.

The flagship and the brig continued to remain in the Mississippi off New Orleans, where they had lain for months through lack of funds to put to sea. Commodore Edwin Moore, as he received order after order to sail for home, chose to disobey. There were several reasons why he took this course. First, he suspected that Houston wanted to sell the navy. Secondly, the Commodore had used much of his own money to keep the ships afloat, and he had made notes for additional funds. And third, he was making a deal—a privately negotiated deal with rebellious Yucatan for the employment of the Texan Navy.

Already he had reached an understanding with Senor

Martin Francisco Peraza, who was then in New Orleans, and within a few weeks he was to receive Yucateco cash with which to provision and equip.

Moore was determined, but so was Houston—and thus was started the second phase of a feud which was to end with Houston proclaiming the Commodore and all his men "pirates and outlaws."

Back in Texas the president, his commands unheeded, fumed and fretted—and then, late in January, he induced Congress to pass a secret act ordering sale of the navy!

This victory won, Sam Houston now dispatched to New Orleans two naval commissioners, Colonel James Morgan and William Bryan, with orders to discharge the Commodore and bring the vessels to Galveston. Meanwhile G. W. Hill, secretary of War and Marine, was to write letters to a Baltimore firm offering the *Austin* and the *Wharton* for sale.

Colonel Morgan and Bryan, upon their arrival at New Orleans on February 25, found Moore outfitting with the Yucatan money, and they delivered to him a communication from the Navy Department addressed, ironically, to "Commander J. T. K. Lothrop, or officer in command of the Navy." It requested that Moore leave the flagship—and Moore refused.

The commissioners then reported to the Texas government:

"In reply to these several plain and positive requirements, the Department and the commissioners were informed by Post Captain E. W. Moore that he had entered into a compact with the authorities of Yucatan for the employment, on the coast of that country, of the Texas Navy, upon certain conditions; that he had received and disbursed money on account of the stipulations of this contract, and that the vessels would in a short time be fully fitted and manned for a cruise, when he should proceed to sea in the execution of the former orders and the above contract, refusing to yield possession of the vessels or to report to the Department."

On March 21 Commodore Moore was again "fired" —and again he refused to be "fired." The commissioners then ordered Commander Lothrop to take command of the flagship and he declined, alleging that he should receive no orders direct from the department.

On April 3 Commodore Moore was placed under "arrest" through the following notice he received from the Department:

> "In consequence of your repeated disobedience of orders, and failure to keep the Department advised of your operations and proceedings, and to settle your accounts at the Treasury, within three or at most six months, from the receipt of the money which has been disbursed, as the laws require, and as you were recently ordered to do, you are hereby suspended from all command, and will report forthwith, in arrest, to the Department in person."

There is nothing to indicate that the Commodore took the matter seriously, for the commissioners, reporting on the arrest, said: "after which he continued to exercise the functions of commander of the navy."

Moore calmly went about the business of outfitting for sea, and it is evident that the commissioners took what might be called "a shine" to the commander, for they allowed him to go ahead with his plans upon his promise that he would take a course for Galveston as soon as possible.

Under these peculiar conditions, one of the Commodore's first acts was to call a court-martial for the mutineers of the *San Antonio* who, with the exception of Sergeant Oswald (who had escaped) and Pumpilly (who had died) still were languishing in the parish jail.

The proceedings started aboard the *Austin* on April 10, within 200 yards of the mutiny scene, before a court composed of Captain Lothrop, Lieutenants A. G. Gray, J. P. Lansing, G. Cummings, D. C. Wilbur and Surgeon T. P. Anderson.

Early in the hearing Joseph Sheppard turned prosecution witness. He described the hatching of the plot on Isle of Mugeres, branded Oswald as chief instigator and Pumpilly as the actual slayer of Lieutenant Fuller.

After able defense by Hugh Short, A. C. Bullitt and R. L. Brenham, the cases were closed on April 14 with the announcement that the verdict and the penalties would not be given out by Commodore Moore until the ships, then ready to sail, were at sea.

At 9 a. m. on Saturday, April 15, the *Austin* and the *Wharton* left New Orleans, towed from their mooring to the Balize by the towboat *Lion*. The *Austin* had 146 men aboard and the *Wharton* 86, and Moore announced the destination as Galveston.

"The officers and men," reported the *Tropic,* which suspected that the vessels were not going to Galveston, "were in high spirits and we trust it will be in our power, when we next hear from them, to record a brilliant victory upon the deep sea over the subtle and treacherous foes they seek. . . . The fate of the *San Antonio* mutineers will not be disclosed until the squadron sets sail upon the Gulf of Mexico.

"We are truly rejoiced that Commodore Moore, after his protracted delay in this port, has embarked under the most flattering auspices. The sloop and the brig bear upon their decks a band of brave and gallant spirits, who will doubtless make up in active and bold exploits for the long period of inactivity and repose forced upon them by circumstances. May success attend their path, and a halo of naval glory encircle the Lone Star of Texas.

"The Gulf of Mexico, during the next few weeks, will be the theater of the most important naval operations that have agitated the world for more than a quarter of a century—operations important in their influence upon life and property, especially important in their influence upon the cause of civilization and the destinies of the Anglo-Saxon race. Two months will decide, in all human probability, whether the Mexicans, aided to a certain extent by the vast naval power of old England, shall exercise supremacy in the Gulf of Mexico and the Caribbean Sea; or whether the small but gallant navy of the Lone Star shall bear its free banner

—the emblem of an infant but rising Republic—unmolested and independently to the ports and harbors of that region. We entertain no fears for the result...."

The *Austin* and the *Wharton* were detained at the Balize by heavy fogs until Wednesday, and during the delay an important decision was reached in a conference between Moore and Commissioner Morgan.

Colonel Morgan's alibi, given later, was to the effect that, while the ships lingered at the Balize, he received advices that the Mexican commander intended to take his fleet and proceed to Galveston and sack it.

Anyhow, Commissioner Morgan, in ordering Moore to proceed to Galveston, stipulated that he should go by way of Yucatan, there to meet the Mexican fleet and thus "save Galveston from destruction."

Morgan warned Moore, however, that the wrath of the president might be a wondrous thing to behold—that Old Sam might even go to the extremity of declaring him a pirate—but that worried the Commodore not at all. He sat down in his cabin and wrote two letters, the first to F. Pinkard, editor of the Texas Times at Galveston. In it he said:

"In event of my being declared by Proclamation of the President as a pirate, or outlaw, you will please state over my signature that I go down to attack the Mexican squadron with the consent and full concurrance of Col. James Morgan, who is on board this ship as one of the commissioners to carry into effect the secret act of Congress, in relation to the navy, and who is going with me, believing as he does that it is the best thing that could be done for the country. This ship and the brig have excellent men aboard, and the officers and men are all eager for the contest. We go to make one desperate struggle to turn the tide of ill luck that has so long been running against Texas. You shall hear from me as soon as possible."

And then he wrote another letter, this one to the editor of the New Orleans Tropic in regard to the sentences to be imposed on the mutineers of the *San Antonio*. In this one he said:

"I have thought it best to give you this information, as in the course of human events we might all go to the bottom."

Then, after saying that he would carry out the sentences within a few days, he informed the Tropic that Antonio Landois, James Hudgins, Isaac Allen and William Simpson had been condemned to death; that William Barrington had been sentenced to receive 100 lashes with the cats; that John Williams would receive 50; that Cook Edward Keenan would receive 100; and that Frederick Sheppard had been found not guilty.

The letters written, and the crew having tried out some patent shot invented by a Dr. Massey of New Orleans, the *Austin* and the *Wharton* took advantage of a lift in the fog to sail for salt water out of the Northeast Pass of the Mississippi.

The logbook of Alfred Walke briefs the events of that day as follows:

"April 20.—At 5:45 p. m. we weighed our anchor in company with Brig *Wharton,* made sail, beat to quarters, shotted the guns, beat the retreat and started for

Telchac, where we expected to meet the Mexican schooner *Montezuma*.

Telchac was 160 miles from Campeche, and after attending to the *Montezuma* there, Commodore Moore expected to proceed to Campeche where the eight gunboats and two small schooners of the Yucatan navy—under the command of Captain James Boylan, formerly of the Texas Navy—were blockaded by the Mexican fleet.

But Moore had scarcely cleared the Balize before the steamer *New York* arrived in New Orleans from Galveston with an extraordinary piece of news. It was contained in an official proclamation from President Sam Houston of Texas, and it read:

"Whereas, E. W. Moore, a Post Captain commanding the Navy of Texas, was, on the 29th day of October, 1842, by the acting Secretary of War and Marine, under the direction of the President, ordered to leave the port of New Orleans, in the United States, and sail with all the vessels under his command, to the port of Galveston in Texas; and whereas the said orders were reiterated on the 5th and 16th of November, 1842; and whereas he, the said Post Captain E. W. Moore, was ordered again, 2nd December 1842, to proceed immediately and report to the Department in person; and whereas, he was again, on the 2nd January, 1843, ordered to act in conformity with previous orders, and, if practicable, report at Galveston: and whereas he was again on the 22nd of the same month, preemptorily ordered to report in person to the Department, and to leave the ship *Austin* and the brig *Wharton* under the command of the senior officer present; and whereas, also, commissioners were appointed and duly commissioned, under a secret act of the Congress of the Republic, in relation to the future disposition of the Navy of Texas, who proceeded to New Orleans in discharge of the duties assigned them and, whereas, the said Post Captain E. W. Moore, has disobeyed, and has continued to disobey, all orders of this government, and has refused, and continues to refuse, to deliver over said vessels to the said commissioners in accordance with law; but, on the contrary, declares a disregard of the orders of this government, and avows his intention to proceed to sea under the flag of Texas, and in direct violation of said orders, and cruize upon the high seas with armed vessels, contrary to the laws of this Republic and of nations: and, whereas, the President of the Republic is determined to enforce the laws and exonerate the nation from the imputation and sanction of such infamous conduct; and with a view to exercise the offices of friendship and good neighborhood toward those nations whose recognition has been obtained; and for the purpose of according due respect to the safety of commerce and the maintenance of those most essential rules of subordination which have not heretofore been so flagrantly violated by the subaltern officers of any organized government, known to the present age, it has become necessary and proper to make public these various acts of disobedience, contumacy and mutiny, on the part of the said Post Captain E. W. Moore; Therefore: I, Sam Houston, President, and Commander-in-chief of the Army and Navy of the Republic of Texas, do, by these presents, declare and proclaim, that he, the aforesaid Post Captain, E. W. Moore, is suspended from all command in the Navy of the Republic of Texas, and that all orders 'sealed' or otherwise, which were issued to the said Post Captain, E. W. Moore, previous to the 29th October, 1842, are hereby revoked and declared null and void, and he is hereby commanded to obey his subsequent orders, and report forthwith in person to the Head of the Department of War and Marine of this government.

"And I do further declare and proclaim, on failure of obedience to this command, or on his having gone to sea, contrary to orders, that this government will no longer hold itself responsible for his acts upon the high seas; but in such case, requests all governments in treaty, or on terms of amity with this government, or all naval officers on the high seas or in ports foreign to this country, to seize the said Post Captain, E. W. Moore, the ship *Austin* and the brig *Wharton*, with their crews, and bring them into the port of Galveston, that the vessels may be secured to the Republic, and the culprit or culprits arraigned and punished by the sentence of a legal tribunal.

"The Naval Powers of Christendom will not permit such a flagrant outrage by a commander of public vessels of war upon the right of his nation and upon his official oath and duty, to pass unrebuked; for such would be to destroy all civil rule and establish a precedent which would jeopardize the commerce on the ocean and render encouragement and sanction of piracy.

"In testimony whereof, I have hereunto set my hand and caused the great seal of the Republic to be affixed. Done at Washington the 23rd day of March, in the year of our Lord, one thousand eight hundred and forty-three, and the Independence of the Republic the eighth. Sam Houston."

But the proclamation arrived too late. Moore, the chief commissioner with him, was on his way to Campeche. Although he carried the technical rank of a commodore he was now, in the eyes of the world, little better than any other among those "brethren of the coast" who sailed under the Skull and Cross-Bones.

The New Orleans Tropic, after publishing Houston's piracy proclamation, had but one comment. It was:

"If the next arrival from Texas does not inform us that the miserable fool who presides over the fate of Texas at the present time has been lynched, we shall be disappointed."

Chapter XII

DEATH ON THE FORE-YARD

Leaving the Balize the *Austin* and the *Wharton* rolled out through Northeast Pass of the Mississippi and reached salt water on April 20th. Then, with shotted guns, the two ships of war started beating for Telchac, the crews eagerly anticipating a duel with the new Mexican steamer *Montezuma,* reported to be hovering near that port.

After months of inaction the men were in high spirits, anxious to meet any vessel flying "the Buzzard and Snake"—as the tars of Texas called the flag of Mexico.

There was a new officer aboard the flagship *Austin,* and he was receiving his full share of good-natured jibes, for everybody knew what had happened to Lieutenant C. B. Snow.

Lately, he had been in command of the brig *Archer* in Galveston harbor, but when news had come to him of the adventure being planned by Commodore Moore, the lieutenant had very frankly informed the Navy Department that he was abandoning the *Archer* and going to New Orleans to join the *Austin.*

The Department immediately charged Snow with deserting his post and ordered him to "report forthwith to the Department in arrest," but the lieutenant . . . who never liked to miss the fun . . . either neglected or overlooked the matter and caught passage on a boat for New Orleans. He had arrived just in time to catch the sailing. . . .

But if there was a certain amount of gayety among the officers and men, there was a troubled expression on one face—that of Commodore Moore. He had what he termed "a painful but sacred duty" to perform . . . execution of sentence on the *San Antonio* mutineers . . . and he wanted to finish the business as speedily as possible.

Let Midshipman Alfred Walke, whose log-book is preserved today in the Texas archives, tell the story of that affair. These are Walke's written words:

"April 21.—During the night of the 20th the brig parted company with us. Exercised our crew at general quarters from 4 until 6 p. m. At 10:30 a. m. called all hands to witness sentence of court-martial in the case of the mutineers of the Texas Schooner-of-War *San Antonio,* when the articles of war were read, the charges and specifications of charges also read against Frederick Sheppard, who was acquitted and released. John Williams, who was guilty, but in consideration of his informing Lt. Dearborn at the last moment that a mutiny was to take place, his sentence was 100 lashes with the cats, and was told he would have it inflicted on him the next day at Meridian. The charges were mutiny, murder, or an attempt to murder, and desertion.

"April 22.—Sentence of court-martial was executed on William Barrington (100 lashes with the cats).

"April 25.—This day beating for Telchac. At 11:30 a. m. called all hands to witness sentence of court-martial in case of schooner *San Antonio* when Articles of War were read . . . and charges also read against Edward Keenan, who was guilty of the third charge and punished immediately with 100 lashes with the cats and released; and Antonio Landois, William Simpson, Isaac Allen and James Hudgins, who were found guilty of all the charges and sentenced to be hung at the fore yardarm, and given until Meridian next day to prepare to die, when the crew was piped down and the prisoners were secured on the quarterdeck at No. 9 gun.

"April 26.—Still beating for Telchac. At 11:30 laid the fore topsail to the mast and hoisted the colors. At 11:45 called all hands to execute sentence of courtmartial, when they were addressed by Commodore Moore on the subject of mutiny. At 12 the prisoners were carried forward and placed upon the scaffold. After addressing the crew the ropes were placed around their necks. Until this time they appeared to believe they would be pardoned and did not evince much fear, but now the truth flashed upon them and they knew they had to pay the penalty of their crimes and commenced praying eagerly and piteously for pardon. At 12:20 a signal gun was fired and the four prisoners run up to the foreyard. At 1:30 p. m. lowered the prisoners down and gave them to their messes to prepare for burial. At 1:40 filled away. At 2:30 laid the main topsail to the mast and called all hands to bury the dead, and after reading the funeral service over them, their earthly remains were committed to the deep. Filled away and stood on our course. . . ."

In a report on the execution written later by Commodore Moore he remarked that during the hour and ten minutes the bodies remained on the fore-yard the crew went to dinner. Explaining his own reaction, the Commodore wrote:

"I shall not attempt to describe to you the preparation or my feelings on the occasion. I had never seen a man executed. The brig *Wharton* was not in sight, and there never was a crew that performed the *awful, painful,* but *sacred* duty with better decorum and discipline . . . Surgeon Anderson read the funeral service."

Thus was closed the case of the *San Antonio* mutiny —with death on the fore-yard.

The flagship then fell in with the brig *Wharton* and made for Telchac under all sail. Continuing Midshipman Walke's log:

"Friday, April 28, 1843.—This p. m. got everything ready for an engagement. At 6:45 hove to. At 4:30 made Telchac. Enemy's steamer *Montezuma* not there as expected. At 11:50 filled away and stood off and on. At daylight the *Wharton* in sight. At 4:15 laid mizzen topsail to the mast for her to come up with us. At 10:30 filled away, made sail and stood for Sisal, the brig *Wharton* in company.

"Saturday, April 29, 1843.—At 2 p. m. shortened and hove to off the harbor of Sisal, when a boat from shore came off to us and told us the enemy's squadron was off Campeche. At 5 p. m. run off for Campeche going ten and a half knots an hour. Brig *Wharton* in company."

Two brave boats moving down to battle—for a contest that would be sail versus steam! One Texas sloop and one Texas brig against the entire Mexican navy, whose seven ships included three fast steamers which carried more weighty guns! Of course, the Texans expected some support from the Yucatan squadron, now commanded by Captain James Boylan, a former officer of the Lone Star navy—but his few gunboats, headed by the schooners *Siselano* and *Independencia,* were small and slow and poorly armed.

Saturday evening, April 29, the *Austin* and the *Wharton* cleared for action and beat to quarters. Commodore Moore addressed the flagship's crew . . . told them that rather than be captured and tortured by the Mexicans, in case the fortunes of war went wrong, he intended to touch a match to the powder magazine and send the *Austin,* with all its crew, to the bottom. His words were answered with a cheer, and the two ships stood in for Campeche.

Midshipman Walke now continues the story:

"Sunday, April 30, 1843.—At 4:45 as day broke the enemy hove in sight, consisting of the steamers, *Montezuma,* and *Guadaloupe,* brig *Yucatan,* schooner *Eagle,* and *Campechano.* We were then standing for the land on the starboard tack, the brig *Wharton* in company, with the wind about east of southeast. At 6:35 hove the main topsail to the mast to let the brig come up with us. At 6:50 tacked ship and stood for the enemy, trying to get the weather gage of them. At 6:55 signal 77. At 7:05 hoisted the Texas ensign at the peak and mizzen, the broad pennant at the main, and the English and American ensigns at the fore. The crew of both vessels gave three cheers. Made signal 76. At 7:10 the *Monte-*

zuma appeared to be aground. At 7:15 the schooner *Siselano* and *Independencia* and five gunboats from Campeche hove in sight standing for us.

"At the same time the *Montezuma* succeeded in getting off, when the enemy hove round and stood to the southward, finding we were coming on them too fast. At 7:35 o'clock the enemy commenced firing at us. Most of their shot passed over us. Some fell short, but none struck us. At 7:50 o'clock manned our starboard battery and exchanged five broadsides with the enemy's steamers, the sail vessels then on our starboard bow on the starboard tack firing at us.

"At 7:55 o'clock the enemy's sail vessels tacked to keep out of our reach when we hove in stays and fired our starboard broadside at them. At 8 o'clock the brig passed close under our lee when Commodore Moore ordered his commander, J. T. K. Lothrop, to follow his motions. At 8:10 o'clock manned the starboard battery and exchanged broadsides with the enemy's steamers, their shot passing over us. At 8:20 o'clock the steamers hove and stood to the southward to join the sail vessels. At 8:26, finding our shot did not reach, ceased firing.

"At 8:35 the schooner *Siselano* and *Independencia*, with the gunboats commanded by Capt. Boylan, passed us. Gave them three cheers, which they returned. They then tacked and followed our motions: the *Independencia* wearing at her fore No. 5 of our signals, a private signal between the two squadrons. At 8:40 o'clock beat the retreat and piped the grog. The city of Campeche S. by E., distance seven miles. Piped to breakfast. At 9:30 o'clock nearly dead calm. The enemy's squadron on our starboard beam, the Yucatan vessels on our larboard quarter.

"At 11:15 o'clock, the two steamers approaching us, we beat to quarters. The Yucatan vessels commenced firing on the enemy; the enemy fired several shots at them and us. Filled away on the starboard tack and exchanged several broadsides with the steamers. At 11:05 a 68-pound shot from the *Guadaloupe* cut the starboard after mizzen shroud about eight feet above the dead eye, Commodore Moore holding the shroud at the time, passed between Commodore Moore's and Lieut. Gray's heads and would have killed both of them but that they inclined their bodies in opposite directions. Shot passed through the poop deck into the cabin and out the stern about two feet above the transom.

"Up to 11:40 continued firing at the enemy, but finding that our shot did not reach them, and they having the weather gage, we kept off for Campeche, the men being completely exhausted, having been at quarters working ship with scarcely any cessation for nearly 24 hours, but in high spirits. At 11:45 Capt. J. D. Boylan sent a pilot on board. At 12:15 the ship struck lightly but continued to go ahead a little.

"At 12:20 the brig *Wharton* passed under our lee when Commodore Moore ordered Capt. Lothrop to steer for Campeche. At 12:30, finding the ship remained aground, made signal 146 to brig *Wharton*. At 12:40 the ship floated, when we steered on our course. At 1 p. m. the steamer fired several shots at us, which we returned, but as our shot did not reach them we ceased firing, when the enemy's vessels hauled off and stood to the S and W, we running in and anchoring off Campeche.

"Loss of this ship (*Austin*), none. Brig *Wharton*, two men killed and three wounded slightly. Enemy's loss—the captain and 14 men killed, and 30 wounded on board the steamer *Montezuma*. The *Guadaloupe* had seven men killed, some wounded, and were injured in their hulls."

While the Mexican fleet cruised outside the harbor, some of the officers and men of the Texas ships went ashore at Campeche. The citizens, who had witnessed the engagement from the tops of houses and walls, gave the visitors a warm and joyful reception.

Commodore Moore called on the governor.

"If I had a steamer here I would give ten years of my life," he told His Excellency. "With one, like the *Zavala*, for instance, I could get to close action."

The governor loaned Moore two long 18-pound guns, which were fitted to carriages on the *Austin*. Then, on May 7, the *Austin* stood out in an attempt to engage the enemy, but as the flagship mast-headed its topsails the enemy ran away, then attempted to get the Texans into calm between the dying away of the land breezes and the setting on of the sea breeze . . . but Moore was too smart for that.

He returned to the harbor anchorage to await a more favorable opportunity. He would soon have it—for the Mexican fleet, now reinforced by the steamer *Regenerador* and two small brigs, was moving in for an effort to blockade Campeche.

Chapter XIII

CAMPECHE!

Emboldened by the arrival of the *Regenerador* to support the Mexican fleet, Don Tomas Marin, on the morning of May 15, 1843, sat down in his cabin aboard the *Guadaloupe* and wrote a letter.

The commander of the Mexican steamer-of-war was in a fighting mood, and the document he penned was more a challenge than a letter. In brief, it dared Commodore Edwin Moore to bring his two Texas ships out of Campeche anchorage and fight him in "three fathoms of water."

Don Tomas, after signing the communication, took aboard 300 additional men for boarding purposes, in event Moore should accept, then hailed the inbound American schooner *Fanny* and asked the captain to deliver the message at Campeche.

The *Fanny* was delayed in entering port and the challenge did not reach the city until late afternoon of the 16th, where it was turned over to Mexican Centralist sympathizers, the officers of the Texian fleet all being aboard.

These Centralists, pleased with Captain Marin's bravado, immediately posted in a public place a notice which read:

"We understand that those miserable adventurers who call themselves auxiliaries of Yucatan, and who merely suck from her miserable population $8000 a month, will take good care not to accept the glorious challenge sent them by the Mexican chief because, should they be so foolhardy, the Eagle of the Aztecs would receive one day of jubilee, burying in the waves these intrusive Yankees."

Commodore Moore did not see the challenge; neither did he see the circular. But he did see the Mexican fleet slinking in toward the harbor, and he swung about for an attack—even before the challenge had been received in Campeche, even before the *Fanny* had made anchorage! The Texas navy, small though it might be, needed no challenges.

Doubtless, Don Tomas Marin was vastly surprised at this speedy "acceptance" by the *Austin* and the *Wharton* at the dawn of the 16th. Losing much of his boldness, he slowed the engines of the fast *Guadaloupe*. The other two Mexican steamers, both superior to the Texas sail vessels in speed and metal, did likewise. Finally, all three, with their accompanying brigs and schooners, hove to and waited. Perhaps Commodore Moore was merely bluffing. . . .

It soon became evident, however, that Moore had no such intentions, and the three "saucy" steamers began standing off to sea. Before the end of that day the Texans would fight Don Tomas . . . not only in three fathoms . . . but in twenty fathoms of water, and would chase him and his consorts fourteen miles to sea!

But let Midshipman Walke again resume the story through the medium of the *Austin's* log-book:

"May 16, 1843.—At 4:30 a. m. called all hands and piped the hammocks up. At 4:45 called all hands up anchor. At 5:20 made signal No. 20 to Yucatan squadron. At 5:25 made signal 406. At 5:30 weighed anchor and filled away, headed to S and W. Wind SE and light. *Wharton* in company. Yucatan squadron getting under weigh. At 6:12 made signal No. 10 to Yucatan squadron. At 6:20 made signal No. 77. Beat to quarters and cleared ship for action. Enemy's squadron under weigh, bearing SW, distance five miles.

"At 6:45 enemy standing off. Beat the retreat and piped to breakfast. At 8 hoisted the Texas ensign at the peak, broad pennant at the main. At 10 nearly calm. At 10:40 enemy's squadron hoisted their colors. *Guadaloupe* at the same time hoisted English ensign at the fore, the *Montezuma* the English at the main and Spanish at the fore, and stood toward us. Beat the quarters. Hoisted the English and American ensigns at the fore and the Texas ensign at the mizen. At 10:55 ship headed on the starboard tack, *Wharton* about half mile astern. Yucatan squadron close in shore, enemy about two and a half miles off on our larboard bow commenced firing at us, most of their shot falling short. At 11:05 made signal No. 968, fired larboard broadside. The medium twenty-fours not reaching, ceased firing with exception of the long eighteens. *Wharton* commenced firing at the same time.

"At 11:18 the second shot from the long gun cut away the *Guadaloupe* flagstaff, which fell overboard with the ensign (later picked up by the *Austin*). The crews of both vessels gave three hearty cheers. *Guadaloupe* hoisted another ensign at the main gaff.

"At 11:35 a 32-pound shot from the schooner *Eagle* passed through the larboard hammock nettings (of the *Austin*) struck the coverings of the steerage hatch, rebounded, struck the deck and passed out No. 7 port, wounding three men (all seriously). Closing upon enemy—commenced firing the medium guns.

"At 11:40 a shot from the *Guadaloupe* cut away the starboard main top-gallant, breast backstay, after shroud, main top gallant rigging, starboard main royal lift, and halliards, and passed through main top gallant sail. At 11:43 a shot from the *Guadaloupe* cut the starboard and fore top gallant steering sail yard in two. (May 17, sea time.)

"At 12:20 p. m., the sea breeze setting in but very light, the *Montezuma* being on the larboard bow, the *Guadaloupe* on our larboard quarter, set the fore fore sail. Put the helm up, squared the yards, manned both batteries, and run directly between them, trying to bring them to close quarters, giving them our broadsides. As the guns bore upon them the schooner *Eagle* tacked, made all sail, and stood to the southward, and did not come into action again.

"The steamers, finding we were bringing them to close quarters and the wind being light, paddled off and took their position on our starboard bow. At 12:50 a 68-pound shot from the *Guadaloupe* came through starboard hammock nettings over No. 7 gun, passed out larboard side carrying away forward port stanch-eon, No. 9 port and the mizen channels forward of the port, with two chain plates.

"Up to 1:42 p. m. the firing continued on both sides, enemy's shot passing between our masts and over our poop. At 1:42 a 68-pound shot from the *Guadaloupe* cut away the main brace bumpkin, and at 1:45 a shot from the *Guadaloupe* cut away the fourth shroud of the starboard main rigging, starboard main trap, and foot rope of the main topsail.

"At 2 a shell exploded overhead, cutting the main royal mast and several ropes starboard side, passed through the waterway and deck into the wardroom through No. 3 stateroom, purser's storeroom, lodged in armory, wounding two men at No. 9 gun. Thomas Norris, one of the men, returned to his quarters as soon as his wounds were dressed, and in a few minutes his left arm was shot off.

"At 2:24 a shot from the *Guadaloupe* passed through the ensign at the peak. At 2:25 a 68-pound shot from the *Guadaloupe* struck the edge of the copper under No. 1 gun, breaking the plank and rebounding, causing a bad leak which was immediately plugged up."

The Mexican guns, some of them manned by Englishmen, had the proper range, but the *Austin* and the *Wharton* stood up to the enemy. Walke's log continues:

"At 2:26 a shot from the *Guadaloupe* cut away the third shroud of the starboard rigging and large buttock shroud. At 2:32 a 68-pound shot from the steamer *Guadaloupe* passed through the hammock nettings over No. 7 gun, killing one man and wounding Midshipman

A. J. Bryant, Lieut. Hubbard, Capt. Cluk and four men.

"At 2:35 a 68-pound shot from the *Guadaloupe* struck keel of No. 5 port starboard side, passed through and carried away both trees, ripped up the deck, injured the main topsail sheet bitts and main mast fife rail, and stopped on deck, killing captain of No. 5 gun and wounding two men."

The *Austin's* deck was now cluttered with debris, but the flagship was giving as good as she received. Her gunners, too, had the range, and they could see that the *Guadaloupe* . . . which was carrying the fight for the Mexicans . . . was pretty badly damaged, and was having trouble with one of her paddles.

The log-book continues:

"At 2:37 a shot came through the hammock nettings, over No. 6 gun starboard side, killing one man and wounding four. At 2:40 a shot cut away starboard main top gallant backstay. At 2:42 a shot cut away second shroud of starboard mizen rigging, mizen top gallant halliards, and larboard main brace. At 2:45 a 68-pound shot came through the starboard bulwarks abaft No. 9 gun above the pin rail, wounding two men, and passed out opposite port.

"At 3 p. m. all the weather main top gallant rigging being cut away, one gun of starboard battery disabled, bore ship to engage the enemy with the larboard battery. The *Guadaloupe* ceased firing and still standing on the starboard tack we, being to leeward and not being able to bring the enemy to close quarters, made signal 81 and kept off for Campeche, *Wharton* in company. Yucatan squadron out of gunshot to leeward."

The *Regenerador* evidently had kept clear of the general melee, and although the *Austin* had once or twice come close enough to the *Montezuma* to give her a broadside, the *Wharton,* little brig that she was, had managed to attend to the latter steamer.

One of the busiest men aboard the *Austin* was Surgeon Anderson. Three men already were dead—Seamen Frederick Sheppard, William West and George Baryon—but there was plenty of material for the surgeon's knife.

Seaman Owen Timothy's left leg was so badly shattered as to require immediate amputation. There was similar work to be done on Thomas Barnett, who had an arm torn off at the elbow. Thomas Norris was in similar plight, his left arm being carried away at the shoulder.

Midshipman Bryant had lost part of his right hand and was seriously wounded in the right thigh; Marine George Davis had lost part of his right foot; Thomas Alkins, Asa Wheeler and Stewart Wilber, seamen, had dangerous body wounds—all these in addition to many who had suffered minor injuries.

The brig *Wharton* had only two men killed, and those by a captain of the guns who had been careless in not having the vent properly stopped on one of the pieces.

The loss sustained by the Mexicans was ascertained three days later—from an Englishman who deserted the *Guadaloupe* and came over to the Texans. The

Guadaloupe, he said, had 47 killed, 32 amputation cases, and 64 others wounded seriously. The *Montezuma* counted her casualties at 40 killed and a score wounded. The Briton said that the *Guadaloupe* was almost riddled, and her sister ship considerably damaged.

Until the 30th of May the *Austin* and the *Wharton* lay at Campeche repairing the damage sustained in the action, the Mexican ships meanwhile standing off to sea to lick their own wounds.

On May 30th, while the crews were busy painting ships, Col. James Morgan and Commodore Moore, while ashore in Campeche, saw in Texas dispatches a copy of the piracy proclamation issued by President Sam Houston before the two ships had sailed from New Orleans. Neither of the officers had believed that Houston would go to that extremity and to say that they were shocked would be putting it all too mildly.

Pirates and outlaws! That put the entire Texas navy in a ticklish and dangerous situation. Why, if the ships fell into Mexican hands now—after fighting engagements without the official and legal authority—every man-jack aboard them could be strung to Mexican yardarms even as the most vicious "brother of the coast!"

The proclamation, by its very wording, gave the enemy the right to look upon the Texas flag with the same viewpoint that they might look upon the Skull and Cross-Bones! And there lay the *Austin* and the *Wharton*—in fair sight of the three enemy steamers!

All hands, both officers and crew, were highly incensed when the news became general. Moore knew that he couldn't pick a fight now, but he did express a hope that the enemy would strike a blow and place him in an attitude of self-defense . . . but the enemy, who didn't know what to make of the proclamation, never did.

Commissioner Morgan summed up the attitude of the fleet in a letter he sent to Texas in a dispatch boat. He said:

"As 'the nations of Christendom' will be on the lookout for us on our return, I presume we will have to run the gauntlet. There is one thing certain—we won't be taken. Our colors will be nailed to the mast head. In the affair of the 30th, when there was good reason to believe we would be overpowered, *the match was ready for the magazine,* an event not joyfully anticipated, but joyfully concurred in by every soul on board. It is not to be supposed that we will be less determined now, when we are fighting with a halter round our necks! Fragments of our gallant barques will be the only trophy for the 'nations of Christendom' to exult over, and when these fragments are rescued from the billows, fragments of other ships will be seen floating by their side—for our last struggle will be a Sampson grapple. J. Morgan."

Even while the *Austin* and the *Wharton* were preparing for sea, Yucatan and Mexico reached an armistice, and during one of the conferences between Don Santiago Mendez, the Yucateco governor, and General Ampudia and Commodore Marin, representing the Mexicans, the matter of the Sam Houston proclamation, and all it meant, was brought up. After listening to the general and the commodore indulge in some gasconading about attacking the "two Texas pirates" as they left port, the Yucateco governor calmly rose from his seat, bowed, and delivered himself of a statement.

"Gentlemen," he said, "in such an event the Yucatan gunboats will be found in the melee . . . fighting for our old allies . . . even at the risk of renewing hostilities with Mexico. But it would seem, my dear Commodore Marin, from what has already occurred, that the Texians will need no help to defeat their enemies."

Don Santiago, a few days later, gave Commodore Moore an extra cannon . . . just in case he might have need of it.

On June 28th the *Austin,* followed by the *Wharton,* slipped out of Campeche harbor. The "Nelson of Texas" and his tars were going home; home to face the consequences—and the mighty wrath of President Samuel Houston.

But they were a jolly lot of "pirates," and they had a new song—a chanty born of the thunder they had lately raised off Campeche. They called it "The Three Saucy Steamers" and it went:

As three saucy steamers rode over the sea
With the flag of the Buzzard and snake,
One morning "two beauties" they spied on their lee
And determined two prizes to take;
But the brilliant Lone Star
Crowned the beauties of war
And the three saucy steamers were driven afar.

And now the bright sun from his bed in the sea
Blush'd redly at seeing the flight,
But smilingly gazed on the Star of the Free
And bathed our flag in its light.
"Come try it again!"
Our men shout amain—
"You three saucy steamers, come try it again!"

Don Thomas Marin was now to be seen
And he called on his first engineer:
"Take the corvette abeam, and have plenty of steam
To keep them from coming too near!"
"God in heaven!" cried he,
"Keep us clear of their lee,
Or the three saucy steamers will be taken from me!"

Our staunch sloop-of-war, with her single bright star,
And our bird-of-a-brig on the wing,
Like peacocks of beauty—are ready for duty
And watching like tigers to spring.
"We're now near enough—
Give a broadside and luff!"
And the three saucy steamers are off in a huff!

The three saucy steamers, two brigs and two schooners,
With Paixhan and Fulton to aid them—
Chose the dark of the moon to depart for Lagoon,
For the shot were too mass that slayed them.
Campeachy is freed
From the Mexican breed,
And our two saucy beauties accomplished the deed!

Sad is the story that such merited glory
Should be dimmed by a tyrant's rancor—
But the victors don't care, when the strong and the fair
Proclaim them their country's best anchor!
So bend the stout knee
To the God of the free,
Who tempers the winds to His children at sea!

Chapter XIV

LAST SALVO

While the two-ship Texas Navy was sailing home after raising its final peal of thunder on the Gulf the newspapers, both in Galveston and New Orleans, were raising a rumbling clap of thunder on the shore.

The New Orleans Tropic, ever a champion of the navy, was especially bitter in its denouncement of President Sam Houston's proclamation declaring Commodore Moore and his sailors outlaws, and it feared the consequences of that section of the document which called upon the "nations of Christendom" to bring the ships to port.

"We learned last evening," said the Tropic, "that the British frigate *Spartan*, 36 guns, left Galveston several days ago, the commander having in his possession the late proclamation of President Houston. . . . These movements clearly indicate a determination on the part of the agents of the British Government in this quarter to aid the President of Texas in his mad crusade against the Navy of that Republic.

"We should not be in the slightest degree surprised to hear in the course of the next few days that the naval power of Great Britain, under the sanction of that infamous scoundrel, Sam Houston, has driven the Lone Star from the Gulf of Mexico."

The Tropic editorially accused Houston of "truckling

with Santa Anna;" it put into bold type certain other things which do not look so good in print; and it published a note which Captain James D. Boylan, commanding the Yucatan squadron, had addressed to the editor. It said:

"Commodore Moore had his vessels in splendid order, and ere this time would have made short work with the enemy but for that cruel edict of the Executive which tied them up."

The Galveston papers were equally outspoken, printing with comment the doings at the numerous mass meetings held for the double-barreled purpose of expressing contempt for the president and gratitude to Colonel James Morgan and Commodore Moore.

The temperature of Galveston citizens was running high. Even the ladies of the town assembled, passed appropriate resolutions expressing esteem and gratitude, and prepared handsome badges and ribbons to be presented to the officers of the *Austin* and the *Wharton* when they should come home from the sea.

The sloop and the brig rolled up the Gulf, and the entry in the *Austin's* logbook for July 15, 1843, shows:

"At daylight Galveston city in sight, W by S½S, distance six miles. At 9 a. m. got underway and stood up to the bar. Got on board a pilot and stood in over the bar. At 1:30 p. m. came to an anchor off Menard's wharf in 4½ fathoms of water."

It was then that the shore batteries growled a salute of 21 guns, to be answered by 21 from the flagship. Mayor J. M. Allen sent a note aboard asking Moore when he could be expected ashore, and telling him that a great jubilee had been planned in his honor. The "pirates" were returning home heroes.

After sail had been furled and the ship cleared the Commodore went ashore at 4:20 to be escorted through the city by the military companies of Galveston, and the accompanying officers looked very fine, indeed, with the ribbons and badges the ladies pinned on their jackets.

Colonel Morgan made a speech. He said that Commodore Moore could not be blamed for the cruise because he, Naval Commissioner Morgan, had sanctioned it. The crowd was still cheering as Commodore Moore went to find the sheriff and surrender himself as "a pirate and an outlaw." Sheriff H. M. Smythe said that was none of his business and he declined to act pending orders from President Houston.

Houston, whose wrath still burned high within him, acted on July 25th. He gave Moore a dishonorable discharge from the navy—without the formality of a court martial.

There was also a similar paper for Captain J. T. K. Lothrop, because he refused to take command at New Orleans on the occasion of Moore's first dismissal; and still another for Lieutenant C. B. Snow, the impetuous officer who had abandoned the brig *Archer* in Galveston that he might join his Commodore for the final cruise into enemy waters.

The Walke log-book for the following day reads:

"Saluted Commodore Moore with 13 guns and gave him three cheers when he left the ship as a mark of respect felt for him by his officers. The brig *Wharton* saluted Capt. Lothrop with eight guns and gave him three cheers as he left the brig."

Walke's entry for the 27th reads: "All the officers in the service excepting Lt. W. A. Tenison and Sailing Master Dan Lloyd resigned on this day and left the vessels."

That was the beginning of the end for the gallant little Texas Navy. Soon the sailors would be throwing their sea bags over the side, and the fleet—consisting of the *Austin, Wharton, Archer* and *San Barnard*—would be placed in ordinary. The *Bernard,* after she had been blown ashore, had been pulled off and repaired.

In November the Republic offered the vessels on the auction block, and Galveston went wild with anger and indignation. Citizens armed themselves and organized into groups to prevent the sale. They pointedly dared any nation or individual to make a bid, and on the day of the sale the atmosphere of the seaport was charged with tenseness.

As a representative of the Republic came to the place of auction and announced the ships for sale to the highest bidder, two companies of infantry stood by to meet any emergencies.

"What am I offered . . . ?"

A dead silence fell over the great crowd that had assembled. The auctioneer waited, and then repeated the query. There were no bidders, save one—the Republic of Texas itself—and so the navy was knocked off to its present owner.

Meanwhile, Colonel Morgan and Commodore Moore

were busy defending their action in taking the fleet to sea against orders. Moore knew that certain high government officials regarded him as guilty of murder in the execution of the *San Antonio* mutineers at a time when he was sailing under the piracy proclamation, and on January 14, 1844, at Washington-on-the-Brazos, he addressed a letter to the Congress of Texas. He told of receiving news of the proclamation while at Campeche in sight of the enemys' fleet, how he had sailed to Galveston to surrender to the sheriff, and how he had received a dishonorable discharge, which literally disfranchised him.

In conclusion he demanded trial—that he might be found innocent or suffer "the uttermost penalties of the laws which it is alleged he set at defiance."

In February a joint committee of Congress, after an investigation, decreed that Moore was entitled to trial. Not only that, they passed a memorial practically vindicating the Commodore. In closing, the document said:

"But whether Captain Moore was guilty of treason, murder and piracy or not, it forms no justification for the violation of a positive statute in dishonorably dismissing him from the service without a trial, or the opportunity of defending a reputation acquired by severe trials, privations and hardships, in sustaining the honor and glory of the flag under which he had sailed and fought. If he were guilty the courts of his country were open for his trial and punishment, and he should, immediately upon his return, have been turned over to these tribunals; and if not guilty, it was worse than cruel thus to have branded with infamy and disgrace a name heretofore bright and unsullied on the pages of our history, and to have driven from our shores, as an outcast upon the world, one whose long and well-tried services, all appreciate and approve."

On August 21st, Moore went before a military court martial on charges of misapplication of money, embezzlement of public property, neglect of duty, disobedience to orders, contempt and defiance of laws, treason, and murder.

The court, after long sessions, found him guilty on only one count—disobedience to orders.

President Sam Houston again boiled with rage. He vetoed the court's verdict, saying that "the President disapproves the proceedings of the court in toto, as he is assured by undoubted evidence, of the guilt of the accused."

Nevertheless, the Commodore stood vindicated—and a hero in the eyes of the people. They called him the "Nelson of Texas" and as such he deserves a much higher place than he has been given on the list of the Texas Republic's heroes.

In 1849 he married Mrs. Emma H. Cox in Philadelphia and they went to New York City to make their home. There, on October 5, 1865, a stroke of apoplexy ended the colorful career of the Commodore. Since historians have so long neglected to give the Texas Navy its merited value in the chronicles of the Republic and state, the name of Edwin Ward Moore is little known in the Texas of today—except, perhaps in that high Panhandle county which was christened for him.

Captain Lothrop, who commanded the brig *Wharton* that memorable May 16, 1843, off Campeche, died in Houston in 1844, at which time he was skipper of the *Neptune* in the New Orleans-Texas trade.

What of the ships—those gallant little wasps of the sea which left their stingers so many times in the eastern ports of Mexico, which undoubtedly prevented new invasions of the Texas coast by the enemy, and thus played a highly important part in keeping the history of the Republic on its even course?

The treaty of annexation by which the Republic became a state of the Union provided for transfer to the United States "all ports and harbors, navy and navy yards, docks, magazines, arms, armaments, and all other property and means pertaining to the public defense, belonging to said Republic of Texas."

In June, 1846, the *Austin, Wharton, San Bernard* and *Archer* became vessels of the United States Navy.

There were no formalities to mark the passing of the Texas Navy; just one final salute of guns reverberating over Galveston Bay—one last salvo echoing its many rumbling peals of Thunder on the Gulf.

EPILOGUE

The following article, "The Dismasted Brig; Or, Naval Life In Texas," appeared in the October 1845 issue of *Colburn's United Service Magazine*. Little is known about the author, Percy B. St. John. It is obvious that he is an Englishman, but his exact status in the Texas Navy is unknown. In the article he refers to himself as Lieutenant, but no St. John is found on any list of Texas officers. In view of the rather incomplete records, this is certainly not conclusive proof that he was *not* an officer. St. John joined the Texas Navy after her "glory" days, and gives an excellent account of the tedium of life in a "dry-docked" service. It is hard to conceive the full extent of the deplorable condition of the Texas Navy until one reads St. John's tale.

The Capt. C_____ of the article is in reality Lieutenant Downing H. Crisp. Crisp was the son of a commander in the Royal Navy. He was nominated a Midshipman on 20 November, 1839, and a Lieutenant on 9 November, 1841. Though he did, as St. John tells us, leave for England, Crisp returned to Texas and took command of the *Austin* in 1844. It was in Galveston that Crisp contracted yellow fever, and died on 3 June, 1844.

The Lieutenant S _____ can be identified as Lieutenant Charles B. Snow. Snow received his commissions, both as a Midshipman and a Lieutenant, on the same dates as Crisp. It was Lieutenant Snow who was tried and exonerated for having deserted the *San Bernard*. Snow, after leaving the service of Texas, joined the U.S. Coast Survey.

The last figure, Judge B_____ is not so easy to identify. From internal evidence (English, plus the fact that he was a member of the Texas - Santa Fe Expedition), I believe the man to be John H. Barker. Barker received a nomination as a Sailing Master on 20 November, 1839. He's also listed as a member of the Santa Fe trek.

Whatever reason St. John had for concealing the identities of these officers, his account certainly concealed little else. Perhaps this was due to the fact that when this article was written, Texas was still a republic. In spite of these unknowns, Percy St. John has left us a valuable account of Texas history.

THE DISMASTED BRIG; OR, NAVAL LIFE IN TEXAS.

BY PERCY B. ST. JOHN.

On the fifteenth day of December, 1842, I walked to the end of the Middle Wharf, Galveston, preparatory to being pulled on board the brig Archer, of 18 guns, then and there to take up my residence for some considerable time. The Texan navy had been long going to decay: want of money and bad management had commenced its career of destruction, and accidents had completed it. The ship Austin and the brig Wharton were at the time I speak of at New Orleans, with Commodore Moore and one or two officers, but without one man even to pull them ashore in the dingy, or cook a meal of victuals. The schooner San Antonio had just put to sea with forty men and a full complement of officers, and been lost with all on board; the steamer Zavala was half sunk in Galveston Harbour, for want of a few trifling repairs; the schooner San Bernard lay high and dry on the beach, where she had been deposited during the awful gale in which her consort had foundered; in fine, the sole representative of the Texan navy in a native harbour was the good brig Archer, to which, my own vessel the San Bernard being untenable, I was now about to be transferred.

A finer brig, a faster sailer, a vessel more elegant in her proportions, and a craft more useful in such a war as that carried on between Texas and Mexico, never sailed out of Baltimore than the Archer, *alias* the Galveston, *alias* the Jim Bowie. Her age was not three years, and not a stick was standing in her, save the lower masts. A finger might be inserted in every seam, her deck let the water into the cabins and state-rooms, and all for want of a little energy and a few dollars. Never did a Government more fatally betray its trust than that which had recently been elected by acclamation, and for which, not long since, the crews of six vessels, fully manned, had voted, to the last powder-monkey. The yards and spars either encumbered the deck and filled up the hammock-railing, or had been transferred to the Wharton, to refit which she had been taken to pieces. Her rigging was principally between decks, where also that of the poor San Bernard was deposited. And not one of these fine vessels had ever been paid for, and will all have vanished from the face of the earth before anything of the kind is thought of. My old friend and companion, the schooner, was within a hundred yards of where I stood, with her deck at an angle of forty-five degrees, and I could not but regard her with a feeling of regret and sorrow, knowing, as I did, that five hundred dollars would have set her afloat again, and enabled us to cruise once more in search of Mexican dollars, cigars, and black piercing eyes, such as those which had taken such forcible possession of our hearts at Tobasco. Many a pleasant reminiscence of scenery, adventure, and social converse flashed across my mind, and I stood in deep abstraction, when a boat came alongside the wharf from the brig. I stepped in, sat down in the stern-sheets, and, taking possession of the tiller, the crew pulled back. All were dressed as common sailors, but, to my surprise (I not being then quite aware of the true state of the case), I soon recognised in the hands who manned the old familiar six-oared cutter, two midshipmen, the captain's clerk, the cook, and, finally, the sailing-master, or Master-Commandant Arcambal, as fine a young Gallic-American officer as ever hailed from Baltimore in Maryland. In a few minutes we reached the starboard gangway, and I stepped on board. The scene presented by the deck was, for a man-of-war, somewhat original. The space between the fore and mainmast,—which, by the way, raked aft more than usual even in an American-built craft,—was entirely filled up by spars from aloft, covered by old sails; strewed about were handspikes, oars, boat-hooks, boat-masts and sails, firewood, water-casks, &c., while a pig, the property of Capt. C——, roamed about, lord of the deck. The eighteen guns of the good brig had been transferred to the fort on Galveston Island, but the Archer had on board the heavy armament of the schooner,—eight 18-pounders and her long Tom. Crew there was none, save and except Hussy the cook, an original, of whom I must say a passing word. Born in the neighbourhood of Somers' Town, he had begun life as a bricklayer; emigrating, however, to New York, he had been promoted to the position of a supernumerary in the Park theatre; thence proceeding to Baltimore, he ruralised as a market-gardener with an uncle of his who had preceded him, until the arrival of a Texan fleet in search of men, when he was tempted by the offer of twenty dollars a-month, and plenty of prize-money, to turn sailor. Two years of service had, however, brought him not one red cent, and now, in the absence of other duties, he had turned cook to the officers of the brig Archer, though belonging to the schooner San Bernard, as did all on board.

Having described the crew, let me speak of the superiors. Capt. C——, an Englishman, and formerly a Middy in the British navy, was, and is, I hope, one of the finest specimens of a gentleman it was ever my lot to meet on salt water. A somewhat protracted mingling with Yankees had tainted him with some of their bad habits, but they were concealed by so great an abundance of good qualities that one readily passed them over. Lieuts. S—— and Arcambal, the former from Rhode Island, the latter from the "monumental city," were by far the most good-hearted and agreeable Jonathans I had yet seen; and Judge B——, as we facetiously called an Englishman who had lived on board some months, was as merry, jovial, and hearty a fellow as ever sailed round Cape Horn, fought under Carlist colours in Spain, rambled over the Pampas, smoked cigars and drank sangaree in Valparaiso, Lima, Rio Janeiro, or Vera Cruz, boarded a Mexican, or marched to Santa Fé, all of which exploits our cosmopolitan had performed. These formed, with your humble servant, the number of the privileged,—that is, those who dwelt in and around the cabin and ward-room. The steerage contained Denis Doyle, the captain's clerk, a merry, kind, obliging, though *tant-soi-peu* indolent young Irishman, a hot Repealer, with whom I had before and since many an adventure by sea and land; Smith, a go-ahead Yankee Midshipman; A. C. Goodall, ditto, with the addition of being as conceited a little Jonathan as ever wore an anchor on his jacket.

When I reached the vessel it was just dinner-time; and to that meal I was shortly summoned. While we are stepping down the gangway let me induct the reader into some of the secrets of the prison-house. The officers on board had all been many years in the service of the republic of Texas, without receiving one penny of pay or prize-money, in part from want of means on the side of the executive, and in part from a misappropriation of funds,—the money voted by Congress for the navy having been devoted by President Sam Houston to frontier protection, and to buy off the more troublesome and warlike Indians. The six months which all, save myself, had spent in idleness on board the brig Archer, had consumed not only nearly all the stores, but the habiliments, uniform, and even the crockery of the gentlemen. Government supplied them with nothing. The navy-agent had no funds. Half a barrel of salt pork, one barrel of beef, one ditto of bread, and certain Mexican beans, formed the whole amount of the ship's provisions, if we add a few sweet potatoes purchased by the officers, from what fund Yankee ingenuity alone can tell. Coffee, tea, sugar, candles, there were none. Yuppan tea had been often used, as a *dernier ressort,*—a kind of *tisane* far from agreeable.

Dinner was served in the gun-room by the cook, consisting of bean-soup, fried beans, boiled pork, fried pork, and boiled beef. Biscuits and yams took the place of vegetables. All ate heartily, though heartily sick of a fare so incessantly repeated, and we then adjourned to the Captain's cabin, where a stove was an exceedingly agreeable adjunct to our comfort. Though some twenty degrees nearer the line than London, on the water fire was very welcome all the winter. Being "one of us," all the expedients which the neglect of Government had forced upon as fine a set of sailors as ever broke biscuit were laid open to me. Coffee, it was intimated, was a gone case, though how we could spend the evening without it was more than any could tell. A stray dollar, however, which I brought forth from the recesses of my pilot-coat, settled the question for that occasion, and Hussy, with Doyle to watch over him, went ashore to lay out the silver to the best advantage. I was then informed that the service—wholly represented by those present—was without a red cent. Not so much as a shin-plaster or note was owned by the whole navy. The government paid no attention to any applications for pay or provender—not even answering the respectful remonstrances of the gentlemen assembled, who, when the San Bernard went ashore, had gone on board the Archer, with a crew of forty men, half a dozen Midshipmen, and officers in all departments. Starvation and desertion had reduced us to the numerical force above enumerated. But as we intended remaining yet a little while at our posts, live we must, and it was quite impossible in a climate like Texas that we should do so on salt beef alone. We had all drawn on our governors (not an officer in the Texan navy numbered six and twenty years) and friends until we were ashamed, as men and naval officers, to do so any more. Besides, we were decided that, as we served the republic, the republic must keep us—how, and in what manner, remained to be seen.

Some time previously we had, at the request of the High Sheriff of Galveston, protected a young man from the summary jurisdiction of Judge Lynch, and kept him on board until he had an opportunity of leaving the country. Perhaps in strict justice he deserved the ducking he was about to receive; but as this was preparatory to strangulation, we interfered. The offence of which he had been guilty was defaming the character of his employer's wife, in order to induce the master to discharge the foreman of his establishment, and give him the place. This, we own, merited punishment, but not a rifle bullet, and accordingly he had been protected behind the guns of the brig. The High Sheriff (Smith), an exceedingly pleasant and agreeable sort of fellow, had accordingly promised us two quarters of fresh beef, in consideration of the old junk which the youth had swallowed. This we determined to claim on the morrow. Judge B—— averred his credit good for a tolerable quantity of wax candles and sugar, and I answered for some twenty pounds of coffee, in return for an equal number of quarter dollars, which, much to the marvel of my friends, I pulled out in the shape of a genuine portrait of Queen Victoria.

"Bless her heart," cried Lieut. S——, " I could almost conclude to turn British if I could but see a few more such representatives of your little Vic. By the way, Brother Luff, you mustn't forget a plug of chewing tobacco."

I answered for the Cavendish, and the future thus satisfactorily provided for in imagination, we were glad to hail the return of Hussy with coffee, cigars, tobacco, and a bottle of Monongahela. As the coffee had to be roasted and pounded ere it was imbibed, we each lighted a cigar; and while Capt. C—— read a new English novel, in one of Benjamin Park or Park Benjamin's piratical reprints, we four (S., A., B., and I) sat down to whist, to the exhilarating music of our cook's Cockney verses, which, when he came to the pounding part—keeping time in his song with the motion of his arms—were irresistibly comic. At length coffee came in, in a huge tin, and was divided between us in various utensils of a nondescript character. Capt. C——, by right of seniority, had a tall white mug, without a handle; I, a china cream-jug; S——, a basin; Arcambal, a tin can; and Judge B——, an ornamental flower-pot. The memorable night which had shipwrecked our schooner, had also smashed our crockery. Milk of course we had none, my whole residence in Texas having only produced a sight of this article on four several occasions. Coffee over, we returned to whist and cigars, which, with some dozen yarns of considerable length, kept us awake until a late hour.

At nine on the following morning we rose to a breakfast composed of salt beef and pork, washed down by bowls of coffee, and then went on shore; and after considerable wanderings up and down the town, succeeded in obtaining all the plunder to which I have above alluded, and we enjoyed during some time a luxurious state of existence, which was occasionally diversified by social visits to the houses of certain of the *sommites* of Galveston, where we made up for ship discomfort to our hearts' content. Often, when our larder was particularly unpromising, we readily availed ourselves of the general invitations received from the Captains of the Iron Queen, Alpha, and Nomade, the two former English, and the third French, and dined or supped on board them. The only American vessel in port we never visited; but from the former we ever received a hearty welcome, which on our part was reciprocated as far as it lay in our power. A short time after my return to the Archer, the yacht Dolphin, Capt. Houston, arrived in port, and Capt. C—— being personally acquainted with that gentleman and his very agreeable lady, as also was Judge B——, they constantly visited on board. For myself, I kept quite in the background; I had an introduction to Mr. Houston in my pocket-book, but I was long since heartily ashamed of the part I was playing, and though not liking to own it, was only waiting for a proper opportunity to escape. Accordingly I made myself known to as few persons as possible. The chief difficulty which presented itself in the way of Capt. C—— was the marvellously seedy state of our uniforms, and a minor obstacle to his visits consisted in the want of a crew to man his cutter. The first was obviated by a general subscription of garments, and the second by going alongside the yacht in my dingy "Greville Brooke," which could be easily pulled by one man. On state occasions, Lieut. S——, Judge B——, Arcambal, and myself, doused jackets and tarpaulin hats, the Middies did likewise, and, with Hussy, we made quite a grand show. True, the crew of the Dolphin considered us a most especial set of proud Yankees for not coming on board; but we sat gravely on the thwarts, awaiting in solemn silence the termination of our worthy Captain's visit, which sometimes was prolonged to an unconscionable extent. For this we generally rewarded him by a good lecture on the way back, though we all liked him too well to be seriously vexed.

Christmas Day we received an addition to our store in the shape of three gallons of brown sherry, when we immediately resolved, in secret committee, to kill the Captain's pig, and give a supper on the occasion of New Year's Eve. Capt. C—— had a decided respect for his swine, and all our previous endeavours to induce him to slay the animal had proved futile. In vain had he destroyed in wantonness several of our under garments, when at length, on Christmas Day, the beast plunged his sacrilegious teeth into a small pile of C——'s own wet clothes, and reduced them to shreds. "I wish some one would kill that pig," exclaimed our excellent Captain, in his wrath, though with as much sincerity of intention as the King who wished the death of Thomas à-Becket is said to have had by his friend. Early on the following morning the deed was done; and when Capt. C—— came on deck, his pig was no more. His anger was excessive at first, but a portion of the animal, served at breakfast, dissipated his wrath, and he commended our resolution.

In addition to giving the supper, we further determined to astonish the natives by firing, at the very instant of the old year's being out, a midnight salute from our guns. Accordingly we set to work, regulated our chronometers, and found the very half-second of correct time, when the manes of the past twelvemonth would rest in peace. The guns were loaded, and every preparation made. Our supper was nowise to be despised as far as the provisions and drinkables were concerned; we had roast pig, beef in all forms, oysters by hundreds, potatoes, sherry, and whiskey; crockery and cutlery were the great desiderata. For this reason we determined not to invite our guests until late on the evening in question, the better to excuse our want of ceremony, and to give our supper more the air of a sudden and extempore feast.

The evening arrived, and about nine o'clock I and Capt. C——*, in Texan undress, i. e., in loose marine great coats, sou'-westers, and two linen inexpressibles, entered the heavy six-oared cutter, and pulled

---

* Since the above was written, I am grieved to hear that my excellent friend has perished a victim to yellow fever.

ourselves ashore on the errand of invitation. On our way to the first house, which we intended taking by storm, I and my companion provided ourselves each with a bottle of Monongahela whiskey, to add to our stock on board. This duty performed, we approached the mansion of the Powers (Irish merchants), the juvenile partners being included in our list of proper persons to invite. We ascended the stairs which graced the outside of the building, and knocking, were admitted by a dingy female slave, rejoicing in the elegant name of Flora.

What happened there, our adventures on that memorable night, and the miseries we finally endured on board "the Dismasted Brig," we must narrate in a concluding paper.

THE DISMASTED BRIG; OR, NAVAL LIFE IN TEXAS.

BY PERCY B. ST. JOHN.

(Concluded from No. 203, page 269.)

THE house of the Powers was, as is usually the case in Texas, a wooden tenement, in shape very much like a Swiss cottage, as Swiss cottages are represented in this country, the upper story being reached by an outside staircase, which, once ascended, the visitor found himself within a covered gallery running all round the mansion. Sounds of merriment issued from within, and both myself and Capt. C—— halted, and cast a hasty survey upon our garments ere we ventured to cross the threshold. We both, however, were old Texans, and having by slow degrees lost our ancient *prestige* in favour of the outward signs of civilization, put a bold face upon the matter and entered the corridor. Flora preceding us.

"Capt. Crimp and Lieut. Swinger!" bawled the old crone of a Negress, amid a general peal of laughter, an emotion which generally followed the dark and antiquated dame's attempts at pronouncing English names.

This was excellent; the hilarity of the company carrying us in under flying colours, though had we shown in St. James's-street in similar costume, the chances are we should have been taken into custody and committed to durance vile as vagrants.

"Welcome brave Navy!" cried the host, smiling at his own vivacious satire on the Service; "be seated and join our festivities."

The company present was of a very heterogeneous character. First and foremost, we in duty bound, must mention the hospitable owners of the mansion, the Messrs. Powers. The Captain of the Iron Queen,

Pinckard, the editor of the Texas Times, with several young Englishmen, who had dared the perils of the main in search of good fortune, made up some eight persons in all; our arrival completely filling the apartment. A substantial supper, composed of the usual variety of materials, graced the board, of which meal we were invited to partake; the whole party agreeing that as soon as this was despatched they would accompany us to the ship. We accepted the terms offered, and joined freely in the festivities of the evening, with indeed so great a zest that we quite forgot for a while the purpose of our landing. Suddenly I noticed that it wanted but ten minutes of twelve, and at once gave the signal for removal, which was responded to with alacrity, and after arming themselves to the teeth, in fear of the prowling *mustang gang*, the whole body sallied forth into the sandy streets of Galveston.

It was a bright moonlight night, one of those lovely nights rarely met with except within the tropics, or on Italy's lovely plains, when the stars and moon would outvie each other in lustre and struggle in the heavens for mastery. Not a breath of air was stirring, the wind appeared as if defunct; a candle would have burned steadily in the middle of the street. Walking rapidly down Trement-street, we had reached Cobb's auction-store, at the corner of the Strand, when a stream of fire flashed in our faces, and the gallant brig poured forth its broadside.

The Old Year was out.

Though angry at having missed the fun, neither myself nor Capt. C—— were so unreasonable as to expect time to wait for us. We had, however, no leisure to discuss the matter ere another broadside startled the slumbering Galvestonians. At this instant a woolly-head was cautiously protruded from the upper window of Cobb's store, and a negro voice was heard.

"Golly! Golly! him Mexican come at last. Him gone coon with poor nigger."

A roar of laughter saluted the old negro as he spoke, and perceiving a body of men in the street, the antiquated and terrified specimen of darkness visible utterly disappeared. Candour alone compels me to narrate the remaining events of that night, during which we enacted the part of a set of wild truant school-boys. But, gentle reader, recollect before proceeding the sufferings we had endured, the wild and uncivilised locality we were in, the utter dearth of public amusement, the want of any wholesome excitement, and the final fact that the New Year was come.

A council of war having been held, it was unanimously determined that we should make a night of it, and treat all our friends and acquaintances to a serenade of a novel and peculiar kind. With this view, Capt. O'B——, of the Iron Queen, procured his ship's bell and a shillelah, while his black cook, who played the fiddle, was also pressed into the service. To these musical instruments were added a drum and a fife. Our intentions may be easily devised from the nature of our orchestra.

Patriotism being uppermost in most of our bosoms, we considered it our first duty to serenade Capt. Elliot, the universally respected British minister, and accordingly sang under his window, to a new tune and with many new words, the loyal "God save the Queen." This done, we visited in turn the houses of all the principal inhabitants. When I explain that all these domiciles were of wood, and further, with very thin partitions, it may very readily be believed that our music permitted no slumber to the unfortunate wights within. Those who rose and good-humouredly replied to our oft-repeated cries of a happy new year, were left unmolested, but those who obstinately refused to respond to our good wishes were entertained by a concert of sweet sounds very far from agreeable. At dawn of day alone were we exhausted, when the party dispersed, Capt. C—— and I pulling ourselves on board the old brig in the cutter in which we had come on shore.

For some days we continued our festivities, which however were speedily stopped for want of material; and further to damp us, Capt. C—— resigned his commission and sailed for England. At this juncture there were on board only three Officers, Judge B——, and the cook. From this date began a state of things disgraceful to the Government, and most painful to those in her service.

Not an atom of provisions remained on board; the Government turned a deaf ear to all our representations; our respectful petitions for aid in the way of food were disregarded, and we found ourselves on our beam ends. To eat, however, was a matter of necessity. As I have before honestly confessed, our credit was gone, and our purses were empty. A court-martial was held upon the Texan Government. It was argued that as the first duty of a Government is to keep its officers, it having failed so to do, the Government should be considered defunct to all intents and purposes. The Government being declared defunct, we placed ourselves in the position of creditors in possession of a bankrupt's property, and voted the ship and its contents forfeited to us in satisfaction of our claims. Had we possessed a crew, and could have refitted, I very believe we should have put to sea, and gone into the service of our allies the Yucatanese. This, however, was impossible, and we determined, until the Government paid up arrears, or supplied the brig with provisions, to pay ourselves and live upon the proceeds of the ship's stores.

Sails, ropes, chronometers, azimuth, compasses, &c., &c., &c., afforded a long perspective supply of food and raiment, and accordingly we began. One evening, a few days after we had taken this final resolution, Lieut. A—— went ashore with a new sail, which had been previously sold for the sum of 30 dollars, to be paid in goods, that is, in coffee, sugar, whiskey, and tobacco. The transfer was to take place in the private room of a sailor's boarding-house. A—— landed, leaving the sail in the boat, and easily found the parties who were to buy the property, but they had not got the articles we required ready, and they would not be ready until the morning.

The principal negotiator in the business was our late boatswain's mate, commonly called Colonel Horsefly, a huge Yankee with one eye, whom we knew to be well-meaning and honest, though something of a fool. Lieut. A—— felt himself in an uncomfortable position; to leave the sail was a doubtful speculation, and to bring it ashore in broad daylight was far from pleasant. Colonel Horsefly and old Mellor, the landlord of the house, however, pledged their words as to the safety of the article, and in A——'s presence it was locked up in a small dining-room, and the key retained by the owner of the house.

A—— now returned on board, much disappointed, but we made the best we could of it, and retiring to rest early were on deck at dawn. It now blew half a gale of wind, but this we minded not, our hopes of wholesome plunder being great. The boat was manned by all on board, armed to the teeth, and away we sped before the breeze, our oars being scarcely required. Landing on a steam-boat wharf, we there found Colonel Horsefly, his countenance elongated to a most alarming and unnatural extent.

"What is the matter!" cried we, with one simultaneous impulse of alarm.

"They've stolen the sail," replied the colonel, with a rueful visage.

"You villain," cried Lieut. Snow, collaring the huge Yankee; "you are an accomplice. If you don't give back the sail, we'll take you on board and give you six dozen."

The counterpart of Long Tom Coffin woefully replied that he was innocent and would do everything in his power to track the thieves. On this condition he was released, and placed at our head, while we with loaded and cocked pistols kept our eye upon him. Our first act was to examine the room which contained the sail; this we did unobserved, not a soul being as yet up in all Galveston save ourselves. We found on examination that the door had been opened by means of a picklock. The colonel now examined the sandy street, and immediately gave utterance to a low whistle, at the same time pointing out the track of three men who had plainly dragged a heavy body along the street for some distance. The colonel now unhesitatingly gave it as his opinion that the three men who with him should have purchased the sail were themselves the robbers, and offered to lead us to their lair.

"Lead on!" cried we; "lead on."

Away walked the colonel, taking huge strides, which we with difficulty kept up with, towards an abandoned shanty in the outskirts of the town. Angry at being taken in we clutched our pistols, determined at any cost to regain possession of our property. The house was in fact not a house, but a hut with a small door and a single narrow window, situated in the centre of a kind of morass, approached by a pathway very little differing from the surrounding bog.

We reached the door undiscovered. Not a sound was heard within, save a low, thick breathing. The colonel approached the window. It was open. A glance of satisfaction revealed that all was right. To raise the latch—to enter and awake the three thieves was the work of an instant, and the three desperadoes found themselves with each a pistol at his mouth, and a knee upon his heart. Not a motion, not a sound escaped them. They were fairly trapped. Lieut. Snow ordered the gang to be bound with their hands behind their backs, and then, they being all runaway sailors from the navy, we made a show of marching them on board to a good flogging. Content, however, with recapturing our sail, we soon left them and returned to the boarding-house, where eatables were speedily forthcoming.

Such is a specimen of the difficulties and indignities we endured during many weeks. It would be too painful to detail some of our after sufferings. Suffice that at the expiration of two months, finding all hope of redress useless, we went ashore, threw up our commissions, took ship for our several native lands, and ceased for ever all connexion with the Texan navy.